UNDERSTANDING
BODY
LANGUAGE

HAMLYN HELP YOURSELF GUIDE

UNDERSTANDING BODY LANGUAGE

JANE LYLE

HAMLYN

First published in 1989 by
The Hamlyn Publishing Group Limited,
a division of the Octopus Publishing Group,
Michelin House, 81 Fulham Road,
London SW3 6RB.

ISBN 0 600 56488 6

Typeset by Bookworm Typesetting, Manchester
Printed and bound in Great Britain by
The Guernsey Press Co. Ltd., Guernsey, Channel Islands.

CONTENTS

INTRODUCTION

Body language can be subtle, blatant, cultural, or related to age or occupation. It is also universal, and forms the basic language we all use to communicate with each other.

Learning about what scientists call 'non-verbal communication' can greatly enhance your life. Socially, for example, you could be deterring friends or potential partners by using negative postures and gestures. Perhaps you are shy, or uncertain about how attractive you are. This attitude will reveal itself in your body language, and send out the message that you are not interested in or available for social contact. But this may not be the message you really want to transmit.

Similarly, once you learn how to recognize when somebody is feeling defensive or uncomfortable you can diffuse the situation. Instead of reacting aggressively yourself, you will be able to coax a response out of the other person and help him or her to feel safe in your company. Ideally, then, body language should be consciously used for better communication and understanding. There are many gestures described in this book which cannot be consciously controlled − such as pupil dilation at a pleasurable sight. Micro-expressions which flit across the face are also picked up subliminally by the observer, and affect interpretation of what is being said. You may try to lie, but an intuitive audience will not be completely taken in by the lies your body is trying to put across.

However, other gestures − when deliberately performed − seem to send a message to the brain, and can apparently change your mood or perception of events. Smiling, and crossing your arms or legs, for instance, are gestures which suggest that sometimes the body controls the brain − not vice versa.

The study of body language can provide you with a life-long hobby. It can help you in every area of your life, and amuse you when you are waiting to catch a train or aeroplane, or when you are stranded at a boring party. It can also enrich your relationships by deepening your understanding of those close to you. By observing your own characteristic gestures, you can also learn a good deal about yourself and your reactions to situations and people. Such invaluable information takes time and effort to acquire, but adds a new dimension to life. It is an exciting journey, and you can make it a positive one.

THE LANGUAGE OF POSTURE

Our posture may be likened to a pronounced regional accent in that it identifies us. Our state of mind, physical fitness, and personal body image are also revealed by our habitual and preferred postures. Sometimes these are so idiosyncratic that talented mimics can imitate a famous person simply by copying his or her characteristic posture and gestures. The addition of the voice is then simply the cherry on the cake, for the audience have recognized the well-known figure already – just as in daily life we identify family and friends by their bearing. So by learning about posture, you are familiarizing yourself with the basic alphabet of body language – and this knowledge forms the foundation upon which all your subsequent impressions of others are built.

Victorian psychologist William James made one of the earliest classifications of postural types. He identified four types.

APPROACH: Forward-looking postures which demonstrate attention, and warmth of personality.

WITHDRAWAL: Turning away, holding back, the opposite of approach. These postures signify shyness, boredom, and are perceived as cold by the onlooker.

EXPANSION: Standing up straight, with an erect bearing – extreme examples are the postures of pride and arrogance. Normally, however, this posture is adopted by confident, dominant individuals.

CONTRACTION: Postures which draw the person into themselves – dejected, collapsed positions of the body which indicate submission and possibly depression or disappointment.

These categories are useful when beginning to interpret body language, for they cover basic motivation and mood very neatly. Consider the stiffly erect bearing of a military man, whose ramrod back betrays his profession even when he is out of uniform. Or imagine a sulky adolescent, slouching along with rounded shoulders and a concave middle. Reverse these images in your mind and the military man suddenly loses all his authority, while the teenager turns from a potential troublemaker into a youthful pillar of society. As any actor will tell you, your posture – that is how you hold your body while sitting, standing and lying down – is the first clue to your character and personality. Your posture will reflect your underlying state of mind whether you are feeling confident, submissive, optimistic or depressed.

For instance, a relaxed, upright posture immediately suggests confidence – we say 'chin up' when we mean 'adopt a hopeful, assertive attitude to this situation'. But by referring to someone as 'spineless', we imply the opposite state of mind and posture – conjuring up a picture of a person who cannot 'stand up' to life. By experimenting with different kinds of posture in front of a mirror you will soon realize the strength of the message your posture is transmitting about you.

Body memories

An awareness of postural messages can help you to decide what kind of posture to adopt yourself in order to make the most of an encounter, whether social or work-orientated. But probably self-change is the most exciting potential highlighted by research on posture. A person's habitual posture, or basic carriage seems to act as a record of past experience – for instance, individuals who have suffered from lengthy bouts of depression at some time will frequently retain the sagging, hopeless shape which typifies the illness. It has become second nature to them, and even when they have recovered their bodies recall their unhappiness. A young girl who has suddenly developed large, mature breasts will often hunch her body forward, and even habitually cross her arms to disguise the offending objects. And many women retain this posture into adulthood, having forgotten the original reason for it. Similarly, boys who shoot up in adolescence and find themselves inches taller than their friends will stoop – often quite badly – so as not to leave their peer group behind. Yet by deliberately working on changing posture both body and mind can be freed from the burdens of past trauma. Some researchers go as far as to claim that this approach can lead to insights as valuable as those afforded by traditional psychoanalysis.

The circumstances of our birth affect our later development too, giving a whole new meaning to the phrase 'start as you mean to go on' – except, of course, our arrival in this world is an experience over which we have no control. Birth without violence was pioneered by Dr. Frederick Leboyer, who believed that the majority of standard hospital deliveries take place in an unfriendly environment. The new baby emerges from the safe cocoon of the womb, where it has been surrounded by warm fluid and all sounds have been muffled, to be assaulted by bright lights, loud noises, and an atmosphere of confusion. Dr. Leboyer believed that children born in this way were more likely to become aggressive or withdrawn – withdrawal is a form of passive aggression – in response to a violent birth. He proposed a comfortable, softly-lit environment which would relax the mother and soothe the infant – providing the best possible start for their relationship.

Studies conducted by Dr. Danielle Rapoport indicate that his assumptions were correct. Nearly all the children born by Leboyer's methods are ambidextrous – suggesting a balance between the two hemispheres of the brain – and are unusually healthy and well-adjusted.

POSTURE AND PERSONALITY

Researchers into the connections between mind and body have identified further, less obvious, ways in which our bodies seem to shape themselves in response to our mental and emotional personality type. Dr. Ken Dychtwald, a professor of psychology working in the fields of human response and body-mind aware-ness, has identified five basic 'body splits' which give definite clues to character. However, these physical definitions must be viewed in context – your genetic inheritance plays a large part in deciding what shape you will be. If you are predominantly left-handed, the left side of your body will be slightly more developed than the right. And your occupation, hobbies, or any illness or injury can change both shape and posture – all professional tennis players tend to overdevelop their racquet arm for example.

Also, as Dr. Dychtwald points out, 'translation from mind to matter and from matter to mind seems to be a kind of circular feedback system, with each bit of information and experience feeding back through tissue and then becoming information and experience once again. So in trying to decipher the language of the body or the structure of the psyche, all we can do is to bring these relationships into awareness and to recognize that at times the chicken and the egg cannot be separated at all.' See if the splits described provide any insights into your own character.

YOUR BETTER HALF
RIGHT/LEFT SPLIT

Research into the functions of the brain has found that each side seems to specialize in different activities, and that most of us are influenced by one side more than the other. In addition, the left brain organizes the right half of the body, while the right brain animates the left-hand side. The characteristics of each hemisphere of the brain are illustrated by the following table:

LEFT BRAIN

- VERBAL – the power of speech to describe things specifically.
- ANALYTICAL – a one-step-at-a-time way of thinking, one plus one must equal two.
- SYMBOLIC – the use of signs to represent things, such as male and female, stop or go, plus and minus.
- TEMPORAL – awareness of time and sequence in logical order; structures such as school timetables are a good example.
- RATIONAL, LOGICAL, LINEAR – making decisions based on the facts which are available; reasoned arguments; logical progression of ideas.
- DIGITAL – using numbers, as in arithmetic.

RIGHT BRAIN

- NONVERBAL – body language; an awareness of things which cannot necessarily be articulated.
- SYNTHETIC – collecting ideas, feelings and facts together to form a whole.
- INTUITIVE – sudden, inexplicable insights not necessarily resulting from any particular train of thought but springing fully-formed into consciousness; the 'hunch' of the outstanding detective; the problem-solving dream.
- NONTEMPORAL – no sense of time in terms of hours, minutes, days; often observed in situations where one is so involved in something that 'time flies'.
- NONRATIONAL – the ability to suspend belief; children display this facility when becoming totally immersed in imaginative games; and adults who respond wholeheartedly to films, music and poetry have also entered the nonrational world of fantasy.
- SPATIAL – orientation in space; understanding how parts of a thing fit together to form a whole.

Nobody has yet discovered why between 80-90 per cent of the population is right-handed, yet this statistic is found throughout the world and consequently left-handed people are looked upon as strange or different. However, studies show that we are more ambidextrous than we think – even if we favour one hand for writing, we may clap, scratch, point and wave with the other hand. And in activities such as playing the piano, or typing, we have to use both hands equally. By trying a number of everyday actions, such as folding your arms, winking, or beckoning, you should be able to see which side of your body is dominant in which areas, irrespective of the hand you use to hold a pen. And next time you are applauding, note which hand is uppermost as you clap – you may be surprised.

It was once believed that left-handed people were mirror images of right handers, and that their brains were actually organized the other way round so that the right hemisphere dealt with speech, while the left became nonverbal and creative. If your mother was left-handed then this may be true, but if you are the left-handed child of a right-handed mother then it is not the case. But left-handed children who were forced to write with their right hands at school often experienced learning difficulties, as they battled to overcome their natural preference. This practice has now ceased in most schools, for enlightened teachers have realized the needless problems it can cause.

TOP/BOTTOM SPLIT
Taking the waist as a natural dividing line, the body can be viewed in two sections. The upper section can be seen as an extrovert – for the functions of the upper half involve reaching out with the arms to express love, anger, to direct others and to perform all the intricate and symbolic gestures associated with our hands. Our upper half also houses the lungs and brain, and so is essential for our very being. The lower half of the body is more introverted. It spends much more time in contact with the earth than the upper portion, and supports the rest of the body, while our legs propel us from A to B. Because this part of us is also associated with our sexuality and fertility, and the assimilation and digestion of food, it is connected to earthy feelings of privacy, home and stability.

Take a look at the proportions of your body – where is the weight distributed? Where do the muscles seem to be best developed? If your body is noticeably split between the two halves, does this relate to your personality? Extreme examples of this type of split are the woman with wide, 'childbearing' hips, and a primarily emotional personality, placing home and family concerns above all, and the man with massive chest and shoulders which seem to be supported by narrow hips and spindly legs. He would be an active, self-expressive type who prefers action to contemplation but may have difficulty with his emotions.

While the split is not always as obvious as this, it can also be observed through posture and movement. Which half of the body seems the most graceful and co-ordinated? Which half of the body seems healthier?

FRONT/BACK SPLIT

How often do you see the back of your body? The hairdresser may show you the back of your head in a mirror when he or she has finished cutting your hair – or you may get a glimpse in a photograph or clothes-shop mirror. But it is unlikely that you could close your eyes and visualize your back view, or accurately describe it to anyone else. It is your front that you identify as your self, the part of your body which faces the world and actively communicates with other people.

Because your back is largely hidden from sight, it may be likened to the unconscious part of your mind. And just as the unconscious contains all kinds of obscure and sometimes primitive urges, so the back tends to get used as a storehouse for tension in the form of suppressed fears and anger.

'I'm going to put it all behind me' is a telling phrase which expresses this tendency in all of us. When we are on guard we stiffen the back from neck to ankle, using it as an added support for our more vulnerable front. But this reaction can easily become a permanent way of holding the body, and ultimately result in back pains and muscle spasms. If you have habitually 'put your back' into life without doing anything to release negative feelings, your back is likely to be a lot more tense than your front. Everybody, but particularly people in sedentary occupations, should make a point of stretching at frequent intervals to help release some of the accumulated tension. How tight is your back? Do you have difficulty in being assertive? Are there any situations you can think of which make your back noticeably more or less tense?

It can also be interesting to look at the people around you to see what part their backs play in their posture. Are they gracefully upright, rigid as ramrods, or bowed down as if burdened with a heavy load? Do these postures tell you anything about their character, or life story? You can experiment with posture by observing the reactions of people to different ways of holding yourself. If you try to sit up straight, with a relaxed, upright posture, you should find that this elicits a more positive response in most situations than if you deliberately collapse into your chair.

HEAD/BODY SPLIT

'Dead from the neck down' is a derogatory description of someone whose sensual nature seems to have atrophied. Yet many of us are completely divorced from our bodies, and live our lives in a state of separation between our thoughts and feelings. Because the head contains the brain, we tend to think of it as the seat of the intellect – separated from the feelings and senses of the body. The head and face are presented to the world, while the body remains private property – hidden beneath clothes for most of our waking lives. Apart from occupational problems, which can create distortions in posture, our reactions to mental and emotional situations can often be clearly seen in the position of the head and neck.

An anxious person will stick his or her neck out, as if looking to see what's coming. This has the effect of squashing the neck at the back as the jaw protrudes forward. A protruding jaw can also signal an obstinate and determined person, who will 'take it on the chin'. Rigidity in the neck is a sign of being on guard against attack, and commonly appears when people are trying to cope with a number of difficult situations. The tension created by this juggling act results in life being 'a pain in the neck', in both senses. A jaw which recedes, and is tucked in towards the neck indicates lack of confidence and occurs when someone is feeling sad, and unable to speak up for themselves. A lowered head is a sign of submission, the most obvious example being the formal bow, but if it is an habitual posture then you can assume that the person is hanging his or her head for other reasons. Shame and sorrow typically result in a temporarily lowered head, but it is very easy for such postures to remain long after the original cause for them has gone.

The head responds to external stimuli in a major way, for it

13

contains ears, eyes, nose, and the throat where the vocal chords are situated. These organs relay information to the brain, in response to which we act and react, using every part of the face to express ourselves with body language and the voice to communicate facts and feelings.

However, it is very difficult to think clearly while moving the head. Try setting yourself a problem, such as a difficult crossword puzzle clue or mathematical exercise. Then try to solve it while moving your head from side to side. The movement is conducive to muddle rather than clarity. Rodin's famous statue, *The Thinker*, is a perfect example of how we hold our heads, cupping the jaw with one or both hands, in order to think deeply.

TORSO/LIMBS SPLIT

The final major division is the split between the torso and the limbs. The torso is like the trunk of a tree, with the arms and legs forming roots and branches which extend out into the world. Our legs both support and move the body, while the arms are used for myriad activities as well as expressing ourselves and touching other people. People who use their arms and hands a lot while they are speaking find it very difficult to talk if these parts are restricted. There is an apocryphal story about a Neapolitan who was rendered utterly silent when forced to sit on his hands throughout a conversation.

Generally speaking, extrovert personalities use their limbs proportionately more during conversation than shyer souls. And highly active 'doers' are always on the move, often fidgeting or tapping their feet when their desire to move forward has been temporarily thwarted. Such people find it very difficult just to be still and quiet inside.

Introverted characters, on the other hand, are full of ideas and feelings but have problems with self expression. They tend to bottle up their emotions, and cannot always say what they would like to say. As a result of constricted self-expression, this type of personality may have weak, under-developed arms and legs extending from a full torso – as if the roots and branches of their personal tree are frightened to venture far from the supporting trunk. Such individuals employ a minimal range of restricted gestures, and until they feel safe their postures are likely to be closed ones. More open postures can be cultivated to good effect.

CHANGE THE BODY – CHANGE THE MIND

One outcome of research into posture, and the emotional meanings behind it, has been the development of various methods for consciously changing ourselves for the better. Bioenergetics, Rolfing and the Alexander Technique are all ways of working with your body to free it from bad postural habits and accumulated tensions. And the most cursory exploration of posture will reveal just how far our posture disintegrates by the time we reach adulthood. Little children are naturally graceful and poised, for unless they are ill or deformed in some way their bodies are still free, and the muscles have yet to set into rigid patterns. Yet even by the age of nine or ten children have developed unnatural ways of holding themselves, which continue to worsen with age. These defects are not so noticeable in primitive peoples, who seem to retain balanced bodies well into old age.

Each of these major techniques for unlearning negative adult postures is based on the premise that you and your body are indivisible. The living form of each human being is the physical expression of the mind and spirit which animates it. Rolfing requires a therapist, for it is a system of deep massage-like movements which seek to break down the muscular armour that prevents a free flow of energy through the body. It was developed by Dr. Ida Rolf, a biochemist and physiologist. She noticed that both physical accidents and emotional upsets tightened the muscle tissue – and that if the muscles continued to hold the postures of fear, grief, or anger for any length of time these patterns would become set. Inflexibility, imbalance, and lowered vitality resulted – and so Dr. Rolf devised a series of ten therapeutic sessions, aimed at restructuring the body to enable it to assume a healthier posture. Similarly, Bioenergetics, developed by Dr. Alexander Lowen, seeks through a series of gentle exercises, breathing, and mental therapy to create unity of mind and body – leading to a fuller experience of life through increased vitality.

THE ALEXANDER TECHNIQUE

But the pioneer of posture was an Australian named Frederick Matthias Alexander, born in 1869. While pursuing a career as an actor and reciter he was frequently troubled by hoarseness and breathing difficulties – which greatly interfered with his work.

Mysteriously, he did not suffer these interruptions during normal conversation. Doctors and voice specialists were unable to help him, and he became determined to pin down and eradicate the problem. By watching himself in a mirror both while speaking normally, and while declaiming in a theatrical fashion, he observed that his whole posture became exaggerated when he was acting. The angle of his head during performance was pressing down on his larynx and chest, making breathing difficult and voice projection a strain. Years of careful study followed Alexander's initial discovery, resulting in the formulation of the Alexander Principle – the way we use our bodies positively or negatively affects our mental and physical state. With conscious awareness brought to bear on how you hold and move your body, it is possible to replace bad habits with good ones. A trained Alexander teacher can teach you the basic techniques in a few months, and obviously this is the ideal way to learn. But there are some simple methods you can try for yourself at home, which facilitate a more positive use of your body.

Look and learn

First of all you will need two full-length mirrors, with which to observe your posture accurately from as many angles as possible. Wearing something which allows freedom of movement, but is not so loose as to obscure your body's shape, stand in front of the mirrors and watch yourself sit down on a chair. As you are performing these actions, see if any of the following questions apply to you.

● Look at your lower back and abdomen. Is there a pronounced arch in the lower back which pushes your abdomen forwards? Is your chin poking out? This is a defensive posture, for the body is preparing to propel you into attack. Do you often feel angry or anxious about situations in your life? What is threatening you?

● Is your pelvis tilted noticeably forwards or backwards? An unnatural tilt in either direction will put the upper body out of alignment. If your pelvis is tipped backwards, look at your neck – it will be dropped down, leaning forwards, and the rest of your body is compensating for this position.

● If your head is leaning forwards, look at your upper back and chest. The upper back will be displaying rounded shoulders, which in their turn are causing the chest to drop downwards, squashing the ribcage. This can make you seem shorter than you really are, and affect your voice too.

- Look at the sides of your body – is one shoulder higher than the other? Is one hip higher than the other? Mothers with young children are often out of alignment because they carry their baby on one hip, pushing it out as a support for the infant. Habitually carrying a heavy bag or briefcase in the same hand can have a similar effect.
- Does one side of your body look longer than the other?
- What are your feet doing? Do they roll inwards or outwards? Can you feel where you are carrying your weight – is it on your heels, or pushed forwards onto the balls of the feet?

You have now taken the first steps towards correcting any postural faults you may have – recognition must precede action, for you will be so familiar with misusing your body that unless you bring your attention to it you won't realize there's anything wrong.

Free the neck
One of the most crucial elements of Alexander's teachings concerns freeing the neck – the junction between the head and body – so that it is used correctly. As he discovered, this is the most important area to concentrate on to improve stature, breathing, and the posture of the chest and back. Try imagining your head as light and floating – like a balloon whose string is your spine. Feel it lifting up and away from your neck and body, as if an imaginary hook was attached to the top of the skull. Now gently drop your chin a little – this will have the effect of lengthening the back of the neck. Turn your attention to your shoulders – are they hunched up, crouched forwards, pulled back? Allow them to drop down to a natural position, and feel your chest and back expand. By consciously freeing the neck from holding any one posture, you are immediately creating an improvement – which will help to prevent a build-up of tension in this area.

Wall games
With the help of a friend, a wall, and a stool you can practise a few exercises which will help you to experience a different way of moving. You can also try these exercises alone, but again a

full-length mirror is essential for self-observation.

• Standing about 12 inches from the wall, face your partner and ask him or her to hold your wrists lightly. Hold your arms loosely, in a relaxed fashion.

• Flex your knees gently, so that they bend a little. Now let your body touch the wall behind you so that your shoulders and bottom touch it at the same time. This may not happen at first, and if this is the case try to imagine yourself standing between two vertical poles, and descend between these invisible supports. Relax your torso, and do not be afraid of falling. Practise this movement until you feel confident, and you can achieve simultaneous bottom and shoulder contact with the wall.

• Now you are ready to use the stool, which should be placed against the wall behind you. Standing with your toes turned out, hands loosely by your side, drop back against the wall. Feel your body weight supported by your heels as you bend your knees from the hips, so that they extend over your feet. Gradually slide down the wall until you are seated.

• Lastly, you are going to learn how to stand up – something you haven't thought about since you were a year old. From the sitting position, push down into your heels and use your leg muscles to help you stand up. Most people seem to stand up using the chin, pelvis and torso before employing their legs at all. As you stand up try to feel your body growing lighter and taller as you rise up to your full height.

By practising these exercises, and noticing the difference as you watch yourself in a mirror, you should be able to do them without the wall eventually. And remember to think about your movements, for an awareness of your own body is the first step towards understanding yourself and the body language of others.

STAND ON YOUR OWN TWO FEET

The hideous ancient Chinese custom of foot-binding is an extreme example of altering posture to influence image. Female children of noble families were subject to this torture, which resulted in tiny, useless feet resembling hooves. Tiny feet were a sign of high status, for such a woman could barely walk and had to be carried by servants – neither could she perform any manual labour, unlike the peasant women with normal feet of sensible proportions. In addition, these useless little stumps restricted female independence very effectively, and reduced their owner's status to that of a possession.

Having both feet on the ground is more than just a figure of speech, for a well-balanced person must have his or her weight evenly distributed on the feet to carry the body effectively. We talk about someone's 'standing' in the community, we 'take a firm stand' on political or moral issues; we can or can't 'stand criticism', and so on. And when we are uncomfortable in a situation we tend to shift our body weight from one foot to the other, becoming 'shifty characters'. When people feel excluded from a group standing talking they often stand like this, while those who are securely part of the gathering stand leaning forward slightly, their heads inclined towards each other.

Feelings of insecurity are also revealed by locked knees – that is, when the knees are firmly held in a rigid position. Try standing like this, and you will notice that although your legs seem to be giving you more support, the bulk of your weight is being borne by your heels. And if you offer no resistance a friend should be able to push you off-balance very easily, for without flexible knees you are not standing in a natural manner. Part of your body language is saying 'I don't know where I stand on this', and to cover your confusion you literally dig your heels into the ground.

FEET FIRST

If your feet feel good, and are doing their job properly, then it is likely that the rest of your posture will be positive. Anyone whose job involves long hours of standing, or who has walked a long way in badly-fitting shoes, knows how our feet affect physical and psychological well-being. By making friends with your feet, and increasing your awareness of how you use them, you can begin to improve your basic body language. Do your toes curl forward, clutching at the ground in an attempt to hold on to something stable? Or do you stand with most of your weight on your toes – as if poised for flight? Are your feet flat or arched, warm or permanently cold? Many people will be unable to answer these questions without investigating their extremities, for feet are some of the most neglected parts of the body.

Try walking barefoot whenever possible, and noticing the sensations underfoot, whether you have chosen a springy turf, or a firm, sandy beach. Going without shoes in the house is also a useful exercise in foot friendship, for it is much easier to determine how you are using your feet when they are not being distorted by shoes. Best of all, try a foot massage which will prove to you just how vital a part of you your feet really are. This kind of massage is called reflexology, or zone therapy. Reflexologists say that for every internal organ and part of the body there is a corresponding point on the feet. For example, a point on top of the big toe relates to the sinuses, while just beneath the second toe there is a point connected to the eyes. Discomfort in specific areas of the feet, they claim, can be a sign that all is not well in another part of the body – and by skilled massage, working on these correspondences, health and vitality can be restored to the whole system. Even if you do not subscribe to such beliefs, foot massage will help you unwind – and give you an awareness of what are, in physical terms, your roots.

DO THE LOCOMOTION

The average adult walks at a speed of three miles an hour. And unless we are incapacitated in some ways we are all walking by the time we are two years old, and will continue to do so until prevented by death or disease. The way you move is affected by a number of criteria – and watching the way people walk can provide interesting clues to their personality. Posture, speed, and the kind of stride being taken all vary, not only with levels of fitness and body type – but also with mood and emotion. And gait can be inherited from our parents, along with more obvious characteristics. Next time you are able to sit and watch people promenading in groups – on holiday for instance – you'll find it is very easy to spot relations by their similar posture and way of moving.

Although walking pace varies from town to country, and culture to culture, a brisk pace and upright posture generally indicate a confident individual who has a sure sense of direction. Soldiers are drilled to walk like this on parade, displaying unity of purpose through their almost identical rhythmic marching movements. And happy people have a lightness of step, a certain way of springing along as if they are eager to move forwards in life. A dejected individual is just the opposite – shuffling slowly, with bowed posture and heavy feet. But the speed adopted in a city such as New York will be much faster than somewhere like Edinburgh, for example, simply because levels of street crime and general life-styles are so different. So always take background and environment into account when studying someone's walking tempo, although you'll find that posture is a more reliable indicator of mood and emotional state.

THE WAY YOU WALK

• Hands in pockets can simply mean that it is cold. But when it is characteristic, it denotes a secretive, withdrawn person who can be critical of others but gives little or nothing personal away. When combined with a slow, disorganized walking movement and bowed head this gesture indicates depression. And if the depression is caused by anger, he or she will often kick small objects – or even imaginary ones – while walking.

• Folded arms, in warm weather, point to a defensive mood – and for this reason is a posture often adopted by women walking alone down crowded city streets. Arms which are more loosely wrapped around the body are providing physical reassurance, for it is as if the individual is hugging herself. Whether tightly folded, or clutching the body, both these arm positions are indicative of uncertainty and lack of confidence.

• Those lost in deep thought walk with their heads lowered, often staring with unfocused eyes at the ground. Such people are not depressed, but moving slowly in order to think more clearly. Since their minds are already preoccupied with the thought process, they do not want any additional data to distract them. They will often walk up and down, like a sentry on duty, for the purpose of walking in this case is not to reach a destination – but to reach a conclusion. In addition, this kind of activity helps to burn up adrenalin – and is a useful way to release any stress generated by analyzing the problem.

• The feature of hands on hips may be interpreted in various ways, depending upon circumstances. Catwalk models often display clothes with this pose – walking with their pelvises tilted forward, hand lightly resting on the hip-bones. The combination of a forward-thrusting pelvis with this gesture results in a stylized form of sexual body language, which seeks to make the garments more desirable by showing them on a sexy woman who is doing everything she can to draw attention to her gender.

• One hand on the hip has less impact, and if adopted by a man looks rather effeminate. Theatrical parodies of homosexual men

21

usually include this gesture – along with a mincing gait – to signal sexual preference in a readily recognizable way. Yet, reverse the position of the hands, so that the thumbs are resting on the hipbones, and the hands are curved towards the back – and you have a masculine pose. This posture has the effect of tilting the upper torso slightly forwards as the person walks. And according to research conducted by Gerard Nierenberg and Henry Calero, people who habitually walk like this are characterized by short, intense bursts of energy followed by periods of deceptive inertia – during which they are thinking and planning. Sir Winston Churchill frequently walked in this fashion, and certainly had variable energy levels.

● Strutting is a style of walking which discloses an arrogant, self-centred character with fixed opinions. The posture is some-what rigid, arm movements exaggerated, and the chin is raised – a position of the head which automatically signals superiority. This type of walk can be very military – the goosestep adopted by Hitler's Nazis is an obvious example of strutting at its most extreme.

WALKING BACK TO HAPPINESS

How do you usually walk? You may find this a difficult question to answer without watching yourself in a mirror, or asking someone who knows you very well to describe your distinctive way of moving. Do you look at the pavement, at other people, or at the rooftops as you are walking along? What kind of pace do you find most comfortable? Do you take big strides, or little steps?

By consciously walking in a more confident way – that is with a relaxed, upright posture – you should notice a difference in yourself and in the responses of other people. When you walk into a room in this way, even if you are nervous inside, people will respond to you in a positive way. Take a look at yourself in the mirror first and you will probably respond more positively than usual to yourself. Because you are more erect when walking with a relaxed, upright posture, you will notice more about your sur-roundings – which will help you form more accurate opinions about what you see. Your voice may improve too, because correct posture aids breathing and voice projection, so you should find it easier to communicate. Breathing more deeply will also help over-come tension and anxiety – and clarify your thinking.

STAYING ON TOP

Stress has become the demon of modern society. Numerous illnesses, difficult states of mind and the breakdown of marriages are blamed on the curse of the 20th century. Yet, without the inspiration often provided by stress, nothing would ever be achieved. A complete lack of stress can make us depressed and unmotivated. Many men die within two years of retirement – it seems they cannot see any reason to continue living.

Nowadays, we are well aware of the dangers of stress, but cannot always see it in ourselves or those closest to us. An awareness of how our bodies react to stress, what it means, and the signals we use to try to protect ourselves from further bombardment can help our own sense of well-being and our understanding of other people. After all, if you're trying to communicate with someone and their body language is telling you they simply cannot cope, you would achieve a great deal more by helping them to unwind than by trying to press your point home.

Should you find yourself displaying the same signals you must stop and ask yourself why and what practical steps you can take to change the situation. Doctors and psychologists working in the field of stress management have shown that gaining a sense of control over our lives is a major step towards lowering the harmful effects of stress and enjoying its positive stimulus instead.

INNER STRESS

Our bodies respond to stress wholeheartedly. Our breathing changes, we secrete various substances into our bloodstream, heartbeat quickens, and normal eating habits change. Scientist Hans Selye pioneered research into stress in the 1930s, defining stress as 'the non-specific response of the body to any demand made upon it'. His research revealed that our reactions may be divided into three stages: alarm, which has been christened the 'fight or flight syndrome'; resistance or adaptation; and, finally, exhaustion, when our overloaded survival mechanisms can no longer cope. Here is what actually happens when we react to the stress in our lives. Whether we're facing a deadline at work or a truly life-threatening situation, we are still physiological cavemen.

THE BODY'S RESPONSE

Cortisone is realeased from the adrenal glands. This protected our cavemen ancestors from allergic reactions to dust, flying fur and so on when fighting off an attacker.

Adrenalin increases in the bloodstream. The body's metabolism is speeded up so that it can burn available fuel faster. Extra energy results and the body is ready to run for its life.

The hypothalamus releases endorphins. The hypothalamus is a part of the brain and endorphins are the body's natural painkillers – similar to morphine. The euphoric 'runner's high', states of bliss reported by meditators, relatively pain-free natural childbirth and obliviousness to injury while under extreme stress – such as fighting for your life – are all examples of the effect of endorphins.

Male testosterone and female progesterone. Sex hormones are reduced. The effect of this is to limit our fertility. A precarious prehistoric life included times of hardship. At such times the addition of baby cavemen would have been impractical, so libido became temporarily dormant.

The digestive tract closes down. The mouth dries up so that no excess fluid reaches the stomach, and the rectum and bladder empty so that the body is free to concentrate all its efforts on the fight ahead. Blood is diverted to the muscles, heart and lungs.

Sugar is released into the bloodstream, metabolized by increased insulin levels. This provides immediate short-term energy.

Cholesterol increases in the blood. This acts as further fuel for the muscles, since the stomach is no longer active.

The heart beats faster. Extra blood, carrying oxygen and fuel, races to muscles and lungs, strengthening ability to fight or flee.

The breathing rate increases. This provides an increased oxygen supply to feed the extra blood in the lungs.

The blood thickens. Oxygen-carrying capacity is increased, as is speedy blood-clotting at the site of a wound.

Body hair stands on end. When we were covered with thick body hair, this might have had a similar effect to a cat's fur standing on end – we would have looked larger and more threatening.

Perspiration increases. This helps to cool an overheated system which is working much harder than usual.

Blood drains from the face and is diverted to the heart, lungs and muscles. Diverting blood internally lessens bleeding from any cuts.

The five physical senses are sharpened. This brings with it the sensation of being fully alive, as hearing, sight, smell, touch and taste function with supernormal acuity.

20th CENTURY SYMPTOMS

Lowered resistance to germs and viruses. Lowered immune response if the increase in cortisone levels is prolonged. An acid stomach and brittle bones may also result.

Jumpy nerves, insomnia, weight loss and exhaustion.

Reduced resistance to pain caused by depleted endorphin supplies because of prolonged or intense stress. Increased incidence of migraines and backaches may result.

Anxiety-ridden sex life, premature ejaculation; loss of interest in sex; infertility.

Dry mouth, nausea, bloating, cramps and diarrhoea. A dry mouth is such a common phenomenon when under stress that a glass of water is almost mandatory on public platforms and many television chat shows. Feeling 'sick with fear' is the result of eating, or attempting to eat, when the stomach is shut down.

Existing diabetic conditions are aggravated. Low blood sugar (*hypoglycaemia*) may be triggered off.

Increased risk of heart disease. Excessive cholesterol harms the heart and circulatory system, so it is unwise to eat a diet overloaded with red meat, fried foods, cream and so on.

High blood pressure.

Rapid breathing. Most people react to shock with an involuntary gasp, and the rapid rising and falling of the chest – almost impossible to conceal – betrays even the best actor's nervousness. Deep breathing also exacerbates the effects of smoking and air pollution.

Increased likelihood of strokes and heart attacks caused by blood thickening to a permanent sludge.

Hair stands on end. Today this just provides an unpleasant crawling sensation as, for example, when the hairs stand up on the back of the neck when we're watching a 'creepy' film.

Sweaty palms, increased perspiration generally. Sweating is one of the most noticeable signs of discomfort and heightened nervous tension, and is unacceptable in most social situations.

White face. Someone who is 'white with rage' is much more dangerous than one who is 'scarlet with anger'. The white-faced person is physically primed for action, while the red-faced individual has already slightly relaxed because the circulation has begun to return to normal.

Exhaustion, loss of concentration, making mistakes. Everything eventually becomes too much to cope with as our system is overloaded with stimuli. Comedian Woody Allen is particularly adept at depicting this kind of behaviour.

STRESS SIGNALS

While some of the body's inner responses to stress are outwardly visible – paling and sweating, for instance – there are other signals which can reveal just how much stress a person is experiencing. These fall into two broad categories: *cut-off signals*, which we perform when we need time to think, or aren't entirely happy or sure about what we are hearing; and *displacement activities*, which are often unconscious habits which we perform to relieve tension. These signals reliably reveal inner conflict and may even help us to resolve it.

CUT-OFF SIGNALS

Everybody uses cut-off signals at some point, normally when receiving more information than can be comfortably handled. In a healthy, well-balanced person this can happen when under a lot of stress in several areas of life, while a mentally ill individual may spend the greater part of his waking hours with his head in his hands – completely unable to face the world. Alcohol abuse, drugs, psychosomatic illness, nervous breakdown and even over-reliance on meditation are all extreme examples of coping with overload. But in daily life we all employ short-term devices to regulate the amount of stimulation we're receiving.

Eyes

When you say 'I see what you mean', it is interpreted as 'I have understood what you've been saying'. This phrase is often shortened to a simple 'I see', which, depending upon the inflection, can convey a wide range of emotions from amazed recognition to resignation or disapproval. So when we don't want to see something, we logically close our eyes and remain in symbolic ignorance of what we're looking at. The most obvious examples of this are shutting the eyes for a second or two, and putting our hands over our eyes completely to exclude the outside world from vision.

Someone who closes his or her eyes during conversation is probably trying to remember something more clearly – reducing the amount of visual information coming in aids concentration. Exasperated people also shut their eyes, usually drawing breath and sighing audibly at the same time, while they attempt to gain control of a rising sense of irritation.

Children put both hands over their faces when they're watching something slightly frightening on television. Sometimes they peep through their fingers for a brief moment, only to retreat to safety again until viewing becomes bearable. Adults, too, shield their eyes with their hands – during exams, for example, when trying to remember where they left something or when thinking through a difficult idea.

Desmond Morris has identified a further four, more subtle, unconscious visual cut-off signals which indicate withdrawal from a situation. He calls these the 'Shifty Eye', the 'Stuttering Eye', the 'Evasive Eye' and the 'Stammering Eye'. All of these cut-off signals make the onlooker feel distinctly uncomfortable because they seem to contradict what is being said – although physically present, eye language is showing that the speaker would far rather be somewhere else.

Should you notice a companion performing any of these eye signals, it's important to remember that it may be the situation itself which is causing stress – for shy people most social encounters are difficult to cope with. Self-consciousness and embarrassment make major contributions to the shy individual's problems with eye contact. Posture, gesture and facial expression must all be considered as well. You could also try to be more open yourself, and see if you receive fewer withdrawal signals from others.

Each of the signals identified by Desmond Morris has different characteristics described below:

The shifty eye
Rapid glancing to and fro while talking gives the impression of a shifty look as the person looks at you, then away, then back again – as if searching for the exit or a more interesting companion.

The stuttering eye
Here it seems as if the eyes cannot decide whether to open or close their lids, which produces a disconcerting form of nervous flicker.

The evasive eye
This one is very easy to recognize. Staring sightlessly into the air, or down at the ground, the person seems unable to meet your gaze for any length of time. Although conversation is taking place your companion seems to be in another world – so near, yet so far away.

The stammering eye
A lengthy blink, lasting several seconds longer than normal.

Ears

There are several gestures which show that someone does not want to hear what's being said. Children often clap their hands over their ears, especially when they want a special treat – such as staying up late – and are resisting their parents' refusal. Adults perform the same action when they are trying to think – hence the expression 'I can't hear myself think'.

Elderly people, perhaps a little hard of hearing anyway, may pretend to be a good deal deafer than they are to avoid conflict – or even turn off their hearing aids when they feel like retreating. Other symbolic 'deaf' signals are rubbing the ear, pulling the earlobe, putting a finger inside the ear, and even bending the whole ear forwards in an attempt to block out noise or conversation which is unpleasant.

DISPLACEMENT ACTIVITIES

Displacement activities were first observed by biologists studying birds. British biologist Julian Huxley noted the odd behaviour of a pair of great crested grebes which, while courting, would suddenly stop and begin to preen themselves.

Another scientist, Nobel prize winner Niko Tinbergen, watched two herring gulls fighting – in the middle of the disagreement, one of the birds simply began to build a nest. Other birds will alter aggressive behaviour and begin to feed – or at least appear to feed – reversing the expected sequence of behaviour.

It seems that at moments of conflict between fear and aggression another type of behaviour takes over, believed to be the next most dominant drive. These displacement activities are so common that many of them have assumed the significance of rituals. A very useful purpose is served by them because they can be used to terminate or even prevent conflict between two people, deflecting energy as they do into an area where it cannot assume threatening, anti-social forms of behaviour.

An understanding of displacement signals affords many opportunities for strengthening your own position during an argument. Your opponent's bark may well be worse than his bite, and an individual whose voice and manner seem calm can easily reveal a nervous interior by performing a few small gestures – you'll be able to discern the underlying truth more accurately if you learn to interpret the signals being given.

Waiting

In any situation where people have to wait for something which is outside their control, they will use displacement activities to lessen the unavoidable tension they're feeling. Doctors' and dentists' waiting rooms are full of nervous people winding up their watches, pretending to read or perhaps examining their fingernails with intense concentration. All these pastimes are performed by tense people who have been forced into a situation which is causing conflict. They are unable to do anything constructive and they cannot leave – although most of them would like to.

Surveys have revealed that 80 per cent of people travelling by air perform ten times more displacement activities than those who 'let the train take the strain'. Aside from obvious distress symptoms such as sweating, or even being sick, people waiting for a flight will check and recheck their tickets, passports, personal belongings and so on. Airport cafés and shops profit from this as travellers eat food they don't want and shop for items they don't need. A highly stressed person is likely to be genuinely thirsty, however, and will need to drink more liquid than usual.

Smoking

Smoking is not only addictive for physiological reasons but for the way it provides smokers with an easy, albeit unhealthy, displacement ritual. In a habitual smoker an increase in stress often increases the number of cigarettes consumed. Nervous smokers may continually tap their cigarettes on an ashtray, or grind them out with intense concentration, or snap matches in half one after another. Another interesting sign to look for is the direction in which the smoke is being blown. As you might expect, someone who exhales smoke in an upward direction is displaying more confidence than one who exhales downwards.

The lengthy ritual of preparing, cleaning and filling a pipe for smoking provides a tremendous stalling activity. Far more than cigarettes, a pipe is seen as a companion, an extension of the personality and a symbol of the thoughtfully cautious individual. Advertisements for pipe tobacco feature mellow autumn woods, restful cello music, leather-bound books and faithful dogs. And this calming, reliable, inanimate friend is what the pipe-smoker turns to when in need of comfort. Snap decisions are not a pipe-smoker's forte – he likes time to make up his mind.

Eating and drinking

Quantities of food and drink are consumed at social occasions, and in private, when we're neither hungry nor thirsty. No party is seen to be complete without something to nibble on – and indeed the very word 'nibble' suggests titbits for a twitchy squirrel, not a nourishing meal.

Perhaps the most extreme example of displacement eating is the habit of chewing gum, which is often promoted as a relaxing 'fun' activity, indulged in by healthy, happy people – all going through the motions of chewing food without gaining any end result.

Other forms of 'eating' include sucking and biting nails or sinking teeth into pens, pencils and miscellaneous objects. Schoolgirls with long hair suck the ends (adult women usually just pat their hair into place).

Yawning

Yawning is yet another sign of conflict which we often interpret as an indication of boredom. 'I'm tired of listening to this uninteresting person' is literally translated into displacement sleeping, and shows a pressing desire to escape.

A barely concealed theatrical yawn is frequently used in this way, but it is not always what it seems. The yawner may, of course, be very tired and genuinely ready to sleep. But research has shown that waves of inexplicable fatigue overcome people when they are faced with a difficult challenge or a hostile situation that they would like to evade – in exactly the same way as certain species of birds will briefly tuck their heads beneath their wings during displays of aggression.

Grooming

Unnecessary grooming – from brushing imaginary specks off a jacket to powdering your nose – is a major displacement activity, and this sort of ritual is not confined to your person alone. Compulsive desk-tidying or rearranging the sofa cushions are also ways of dispersing nervous energy at a time when to be inactive would be unbearable.

Other signs of inner turmoil include twiddling your thumbs or tapping your feet – both these movements indicate stress, and the foot-tapper may be symbolically walking or running to another, more tranquil destination.   •

Warning signs

If you find yourself, or someone close to you, displaying a noticeable number of any of these activities, it would be sensible to ask a few questions. High levels of boredom, frustration and general stress are damaging influences in our lives. Remember, too, that lack of excitement is just as stressful as too much.

The world-famous Holmes-Rahé Scale, first published in 1967, lists over 40 life events, complete with 'scores' of the amount of stress they cause. The effects of these events may last as long as two years. As might be expected, the death of a husband or wife rated as the most stressful event, followed by divorce. Yet events as pleasant as a holiday, Christmas or getting married are also stressors. Even a great achievement may prove stressful to some people – especially those who find it difficult to relax.

COPING WITH STRESS – MOMENTS TO UNWIND

Everyone needs to relax or rest for short periods during the day's activities. As we are often in situations where we're unable to flop out completely, we have developed other ways of unwinding momentarily. Leaning and sitting, for instance, are two ways of temporarily relieving our bodies of strain – but these actions can tell others quite a lot about our personality and mood as well.

Leaning

It is probably hardest to relax while standing up, for even though we have been upright for thousands of years it is still an effort to stay vertical for long periods of time. This is perhaps why people often lean against walls, lamp-posts or any other firm vertical support they can find. We also shift our weight from one side of the body to the other, balancing the strain of standing in this way.

The exhortation to 'stand up straight' ignores our need for rest, and instead demands an alert posture – which also suggests respect for others, despite personal discomfort. Leaning on something while talking to another person can indicate that we are firmly on home ground – such as in the case of the farmer leaning on the gate while giving directions to hopelessly lost travellers. It can also indicate that we know the other person pretty well, and are unlikely to give offence by not appearing fully alert.

Sitting

'Please take a seat' is a phrase commonly used in situations where people do not know one another very well, but where the person issuing the invitation wants us to assume a more relaxed position. And 'Do sit down' is one of the very first things a host will suggest to a guest. What follows next can be very revealing.

For example, if someone sits down and promptly folds their arms and legs they are not at peace with themselves – they're erecting a barrier. Behind this self-created shield they feel safe, but you're bound to feel that they're holding back or even feeling actively hostile towards you. If their lower body is pointing away from you towards the nearest exit you may be sure that the person would definitely prefer to be somewhere else.

However, unless you are dealing with someone very aware of posture, such as a dancer or a person who has studied the Alexander Technique, it is unwise to try and read too much into crossed legs. Women are often taught to cross their legs in order to appear more feminine, and to a certain extent men cross their legs just because everyone else does. Men as well as women cross their ankles too – although women may also wrap one foot around their lower calf, which is something men don't do. A negative attitude is far more reliably revealed by crossed arms, and even then it is important to remember that the person could be very shy and wanting to protect themselves until they feel it's safe to come out of their shell.

At the other extreme, a person who slumps or sprawls across a chair may be appearing relaxed to the point of rudeness. Unless you know someone very well, you expect a certain amount of attention. Imagine how you would feel if someone you hadn't met before slung one leg over the arm of a chair, and slumped forward allowing their body to go slack. You would feel surprised, offended and less than keen to pursue the friendship.

Probably the most appealing posture to adopt when talking to people is one which shows an open personality: legs side by side, not tightly clamped together, with hands resting loosely in the lap or perhaps being used from time to time to underline what is being said. But this posture is remarkably difficult to maintain for any length of time when you feel you're on uncertain territory.

Next time you're in an important meeting, spending time in an unfamiliar home or even on the train, try to sit calmly without crossing any of your limbs. Sooner or later your natural vulnerability and desire to protect yourself will assert itself and you will experience an irresistible urge to cross or fold something. If you cross your arms you're protecting your upper body from attack – unless you're feeling very cold; if you cross your legs you're protecting your genitals – unless, of course, you need to visit a lavatory!

It is worthwhile persisting with this experiment, for research conducted in the United States of America indicated that students who were asked to sit through an entire lecture, maintaining an open posture throughout, absorbed 38 per cent more information than those who were instructed to sit with their arms and legs firmly crossed.

It seems that a defensive body posture may actually inhibit us from receiving beneficial knowledge – both factual and emotional – while an open posture facilitates absorption of such knowledge.

Ground level
In Western society we spend most of our seated lives on chairs, but before the invention of chairs we sat on the ground. Of course, school children still sit on the floor during some parts of their day – and a massive return to sitting on the ground came with the hippy movement of the late 1960s. Perhaps this was an imitation of the Indian cross-legged meditation poses, known as lotus postures or asanas. Yogis maintain that the practice of meditation is facilitated by adopting positions in which the spine is held erect so that the psychic energies – which they believe flow through the channels of the spine – may freely move from the base of the spine to the brain.

During such deep, introspective practices it is also important not to move the body around but to keep the head erect and the trunk still; as a consequence, these crossed-legged poses evolved as meditation aids.

Most of us who are used to sitting on chairs from a very early age find any kind of squat or cross-legged posture difficult. This is because our knees and hip joints become stiff with constantly pointing forwards, and rarely being turned out in daily life. It's a good idea to try and sit on the floor for a little while every day, perhaps while watching television, in order to counteract this progressive stiffness.

Lying down

At last we succumb to the force of gravity and lie down – the most relaxed posture of all which frees the body from supporting the weight of the head, and from the complicated balancing act which is necessary the rest of the time. Just as sitting in a very casual fashion may be seen as offensive, lying down during a social event may be interpreted as quite a dominant thing to do. Aristocratic banquets in ancient Rome were conducted with all the guests lying in a semi-prone position while servants waited upon them and, although their bodies were lower than those of the slaves, they were dominant – simply because they were comfortable.

Unless you prop yourself up on one elbow and are able to see your companion, it's a very difficult position in which to maintain a conversation effectively for you cannot read the other person's body language. Without this vital non-verbal information it can become impossible to gauge others' reactions – not many in-depth discussions take place while sunbathing! However, some schools of classic psychotherapy encourage the patient to lie down on a comfortable couch in order to facilitate revelations from deep within the psyche, for as the patient relaxes he or she is not distracted by anything external, and is usually unable to see the therapist. A stream-of-consciousness monologue is therefore far easier under such circumstances.

Yet we also prostrate ourselves with grief, religious fervour and impotent, childish rage. In these instances we are behaving submissively and literally turning ourselves into doormats, hence the phrases, 'I'm not going to take this lying down' and 'I'm not going to let you walk all over me'. But those who are torn apart by grief, or humbling themselves before a deity, usually lie face down with eyes closed, thereby cutting themselves off from everything; while children having a temper tantrum are just as likely to lie on their backs kicking their legs in the air and opening their eyes from time to time – to see if there is any reaction to their display.

RELAXATION

Relaxation is essential in our lives if we are to be happy, healthy individuals. Reducing muscle tension, anxiety and stress-related disorders improves our mental alertness, energy levels and sleep. A relaxed person is likely to live a longer and fuller life, have fewer accidents, feel more self-confident, cope better with pain and deal more effectively with those individuals encountered who are not relaxed.

Free the body from unnecessary tension and you can free your mind too. Indeed mind and body are so closely allied that they cannot help but affect each other. Prove it to yourself by closing your eyes and imagining you are holding a lemon in your hand. Smell the fruit, feel its texture beneath your fingers – then bite firmly into it, sinking your teeth into the sharp, juicy flesh. If you have done this exercise correctly your mouth will now be full of saliva. This is an example of how the mind controls the body. Many techniques exist for relaxing the body which will in their turn relax an over-active mind, and some disciplines use both physical relaxation and mental imagery to promote a state of peace.

Pavlov's classic experiment with dogs is another good example of how it is possible to learn to respond to certain stimuli. Ivan Petrovich Pavlov was a Russian behavioural scientist who used the inbred response of salivating at the prospect of food. Over and over again he fed the dogs, synchronizing the feeding with the ringing of a bell until eventually the dogs learned to salivate when the bell rang – even when there was no food in evidence. This proved that automatic behaviour can be conditioned and controlled, and a great deal of subsequent research has been conducted in this field.

Biofeedback, autogenic training, meditation and simple relaxation are all effective methods for combating stress. Although such techniques as biofeedback need to be taught by an instructor, there is still a great deal you can do for yourself at home to improve your mental and physical health – and probably increase your positive body language as well. If you are going through your daily life with a tense body, clenched jaw and permanent frown, you are not giving the best impression. You are also expending an enormous amount of energy keeping yourself in this state – energy which could undoubtedly be put to better use and enhance your enjoyment of being alive.

Simple muscular exercises
If you are very tense, and especially if you can feel the tension in any part of your body, it's a good idea to take some physical exercise before attempting any passive methods. Something as

straightforward as a brisk walk can reduce anxiety levels and help use up excess adrenalin. An increase in noradrenaline – a neurotransmitter which makes you feel cheerful and optimistic – has also been found to coincide with regular exercise. The same applies to beta-endorphins, which calm and uplift the mind and reduce depression.

In Hatha Yoga there is a posture called Salvasasana, or the Dead Man, and it is the basis of all simple muscular techniques for quieting the body. With regular practice you should be able to achieve complete relaxation. Here is an effective routine for progressively relaxing the body.

Choose a quiet, warm room where you are unlikely to be interrupted. If you want to relax before going to sleep perform the exercise in bed. Lie down wherever you are comfortable – if on the floor you may need a cushion under you knees to relieve the strain on the spine.

Direct your attention on your toes and slowly curl them up. Notice how they feel while they are tensed, then let them go. Next, flex them towards you, hold for a moment, then relax.

Now move up to your calf muscles. Stretch the legs away from you until you can feel a slight pull, hold, then relax.

Press your knees and thighs together; notice how your thigh muscles tighten as you do this. Now relax your legs. At this point you may tell yourself that your feet and legs are fully relaxed.

Now move up to the torso and clench your buttocks together firmly – a great deal of hidden tension is often stored in this part of the body. Relax and unclench your bottom.

Turn your attention to your abdomen. Push out your tummy until it is a round dome, then pull your navel back towards the spine trying to flatten the dome. This will be more effective if you breathe in as you push out your tummy and breathe out as you suck it in. Say to yourself, 'My tummy is now fully relaxed.'

Now direct your attention to your spine – often full of tension, especially in people who are putting up a brave front. Gently arch your back, keeping your bottom and shoulders on the floor or bed, then release the stretch. Tilt your pelvis back until your lower back presses into the floor and lengthens.

Now make each hand into a tight fist and squeeze a couple of times before relaxing. Stretch your arms out; try to feel them lengthening until your shoulders are stretched too. Hold the stretch for a moment, then let your arms flop down at your sides. Let your hands fall open, palms upwards.

Next concentrate on the neck and shoulders. Pull your shoulder-blades together slowly, noticing how the muscles are working to do this, then relax. Equally slowly, shrug your shoulders up towards your ears a couple of times, then let them go. Press the back of your head into the bed, then slowly and gently pull your shoulders down until you feel your neck lengthening. Tilt your head from side to side until you feel a slight pull, release it and relax. Tell yourself, 'My neck and shoulders are fully relaxed.'

Your face may give you a few surprises as you begin to relax it, for it is often a storehouse of unreleased aggression, fear and unconscious tension. Getting to know your facial muscles will help you learn to control this, and improve your facial expressions. A relaxed face looks younger and more appealing, and is less likely to produce unattractive wrinkles which clearly signal your prevailing temperament even when you're feeling carefree.

Begin by paying close attention to your breathing. Is it shallow and quick, uneven or barely there? Try to breathe slowly and rhythmically. If you find this difficult, count to three while breathing in, hold your breath for the count of three, then breathe out to the count of three. (Do not breathe too deeply for this can create an 'oxygen high' which makes you feel nauseous and light-headed.) Imagine that you are breathing out all your troubles, and breathing in peace and tranquillity.

Now raise your eyebrows as high as you can, then release until you can feel a softening of your forehead. Frown hard, then release. This is one way to stop yourself frowning unconsciously.

Squeeze your eyes shut in an exaggerated way a couple of times; let the eyes roll gently back in their sockets. Now slacken your jaw by opening your mouth a little and moving the lower jaw around from side to side. Keeping your teeth apart, feel your cheeks go soft. If your tongue is still firmly glued to the roof of your mouth, release it so that it spreads out naturally behind your bottom teeth.

Feel your entire body sinking into the bed, warm and heavy, and tell yourself that you are now fully relaxed and at peace with yourself and the world. If you are not planning to sleep after doing this exercise, do not get up suddenly. Your blood pressure will probably have dropped and your circulation slowed down, so any sudden movement could make you feel dizzy.

Mental magic

As we have seen, mind and body are inextricably linked – and if you have a particularly active mind you may need to give it something to do while you are relaxing. There are many excellent meditation techniques designed to increase inner awareness and a sense of well-being. Many originated in the East and were first brought to the attention of Westerners in the 1960s. Some techniques involve exercise and are a form of active meditation, such as Yoga or the continuous flowing movements of Chinese T'ai Ch'i. But such familiar activities as knitting, painting pictures, gardening and cooking can also be a form of meditation because they give you something outside yourself to concentrate on. Listening to soothing music or watching an aquarium full of fish can also reduce anxiety and promote a state of calmness.

In exploring mental techniques it is important to use your imagination and decide what is right for you. If you're a visual person you'll have little difficulty in imagining a pleasant landscape which you can wander through at will, making it a special place you can visit in your mind when you are stressed. Or simply 'see' a calming colour, such as deep blue, in your mind's eye. There's a wealth of books, meditation tapes and classes on offer should you decide to explore this fascinating world a little further.

SLEEP – THE ULTIMATE RELAXATION

'Sleep that knits up the ravelled sleeve of care.
The death of each day's life, sore labour's bath,
Balm of hurt minds, great nature's second course,
Chief nourisher in life's feast.'

Macbeth, William Shakespeare.

Sleep is the most natural, universally available remedy against stress and distress that we possess. Sufficient quantities of refreshing rest promote better health and vitality, and improve our ability to function well in an increasingly confusing world.

Human beings spend nearly a third of their lives asleep. Yet, despite copious research into the physiology and psychology of sleep, we still know very little about it. However, deprive people of sleep for three days and they will begin to hallucinate as if they had taken a mind-bending drug such as LSD. Research into serious sleep deprivation has shown that if the experiment is prolonged people will become victims of paranoid delusions after about 100 hours of wakefulness. Terrified volunteers become disorientated and eventually unable to resist the urge to sleep and dream. For without sleep the brain is unable to function efficiently and seems to be affected long before the body shows much deterioration.

So what is sleep? Physically, sleep is a state in which we close our eyes, breathing and heartbeat slow down, digestive processes diminish and our brainwaves become progressively longer and slower as they descend from the alpha waves of full consciousness to the delta waves of one to three cycles per second which characterize deep sleep.

Our internal clock

Every living creature responds instinctively to the regular alternating pattern of day and night. This diurnal rhythm creates the 24-hour structure which naturally regulates our bodies. In 1960 a medical physiologist, Franz Halberg, created the term 'circadian' – meaning that which lasts for a day – to describe these rhythms which result from the earth's orbit round the sun. An inbuilt biological clock ticks away inside all of us, organizing our bodies' cycle of sleep and activity.

If you have ever worked on a night-shift or flown across a number of time zones you will be aware of this hard-to-alter internal timepiece. These rhythms exist in close partnership with part of the brain stem called the reticular formation – which lies at the base of the brain and activates the central nervous system – and the cortex or 'thinking' part of the brain. Messages sent from the brain stem via the cortex to the spinal cord and nervous system keep us awake. When these signals cease the cortex slows down, and mind and body become drowsy and ready for sleep. Any kind of over-stimulation, from a late-night cup of coffee to an over-worried mind, can make sleep seem elusive. Those monotonous, traditionally recommended sheep might help insomniacs simply because repetitive actions appear to promote drowsiness.

How much sleep?

For the first three days of life outside our mother's womb we sleep for an average of 16 hours out of 24. By the time we reach old age, about six hours seem sufficient. As adults, the standard seven and a half to eight hours is usual – and during these hours a great deal of activity takes place. We change our sleeping position as many as 70 times in order to avoid cramping our muscles. We may walk, talk, cry, even experience full sexual arousal.

Individual sleep quotas vary. Four per cent of people (including Prime Minister Margaret Thatcher) naturally require less than five and a half hours a night. Another four per cent regularly need more than ten hours. Research indicates that short sleepers spend more time in deep 'orthodox' sleep than Rip van Winkles, which may demonstrate that it is the deep, inert sleep which is needed for health maintenance.

There may be a link between sleeping and waking personalities – short sleepers tend to have high physical energy levels, are hard-working, practical, extroverted and ambitious. Those of us who need to sleep more than nine hours each night are likely to be unconventional, introverted and more creatively inclined.

Types of sleep
Sleep researchers have used electroencephalographs (EEG) to discover what happens to us while we sleep. This equipment registers electrical activity within the brain and has revealed two quite distinct forms of sleep which have been named orthodox and paradoxical sleep.

Orthodox sleep has been divided into four separate stages of brainwave activity. The first phase is a light semi-sleep during which the brainwaves begin to slow down, along with the pulse and breathing – which become more regular. It is very easy to wake someone during this stage as they are just drifting off and may still be partly conscious of their thoughts and outside noises or light. The second and third stages see a progressive deep relaxation taking place as the muscles relax, and heart and breathing rates continue to decrease. By phase four we are deeply unconscious and have entered the deepest level of sleep. The long, slow delta waves seem to denote the reduction of all mental activity.

Orthodox sleep normally lasts for about two hours when we first fall asleep, after which we move into the first of four or five periods of paradoxical sleep – the most fascinating and puzzling state of all. Experiments have established that dreams are essential to mental and physical well-being; when people are denied dream-sleep they soon become quite disturbed.

40

Paradoxical sleep – the dream state

For about one and a half hours every night we enter a mysterious sleep state called paradoxical sleep during which – whether we remember it or not – we are dreaming. Our brainwave patterns begin to move rapidly and irregularly, as they do when we are awake. Heartbeat and blood pressure become agitated and irregular and our eyes move rapidly behind their lids as if watching something, which has given rise to the term 'rapid eye movement' or REM sleep. However, it's unlikely that we are watching anything in the sighted sense of the word, for people who have been blind since birth also produce these darting movements.

But despite all this activity, there is a dramatic loss of muscle tone which almost amounts to paralysis. When you are having a particularly horrible nightmare and feel unable to run away, you may be sensing this complete muscular relaxation. People who have used up a lot of energy during the day – either mental or physical – seem to need more paradoxical sleep than others.

Theories abound about the purpose of dreams: one of their functions seems to be a sorting process whereby all the information we have accumulated during the day is assessed and filed away. Repressed emotions, inner changes and all kinds of inspiration are also connected with our dream lives. And 'sleeping on it' can often resolve problems which seem insoluble by day.

Benefits of sleep

Soon after falling asleep our body cells begin to divide at a much faster rate than before, providing almost every part of the body with an opportunity to repair and renew itself. High levels of what is known as 'growth hormone' are released into the bloodstream during the deepest stage of orthodox sleep. We need deep sleep to restore and regenerate our bodies, while dream sleep seems to restore mental harmony. One reason why insomniacs feel deprived of sleep is because the recurring 90-minute cycle of deep rest and inner mental activity is broken by a restless night.

Failure to achieve the deepest level of sleep prevents the growth hormone's release, for sleeping lightly doesn't appear to trigger its entry into the bloodstream. Poor sleepers have also been found to be much more physically active during sleep, moving about 70 times between 1.30 am and 5.30 am, compared with a 'normal' sleeper who will move about 40 times during these hours.

THE BODY LANGUAGE OF SLEEP

Posture and gesture do not suddenly cease when we close our eyes and settle down to sleep. And although we all move many times throughout the night, research shows that we tend to adopt a favourite sleeping position which we return to night after night. These positions shed some light on the personality and can also give clues to the amount of stress we are under.

For example, New York psychiatrist Dr. Christian Ansbach observed that some of his theatrical clients were deeply affected during sleep by what was happening in their professional lives. 'One particular actor was so scared during the rehearsal period, and so dreadfully insecure about his performance, that he would wake in the morning curled into a tight ball – his whole body under the clothes at the foot of the bed where his feet should be. And yet, just as soon as he had received a standing ovation and good press notices, his whole sleeping attitude changed. He would lie on his back, his head supported by two or three pillows, and sleep a superbly relaxed sleep with a big, contented smile on his face.'

Other sleep researchers have drawn similar conclusions and confirm that the dominant sleep posture is linked with our waking lives but can be changed temporarily by feelings of anxiety. Some psychiatrists believe that the real cause of sleeplessness is not so much mental as physical. When we are deeply worried our fears penetrate the subconscious mind, which will do its best to sort them out while we are asleep. But because we are uneasy our bodies will assume a new, self-protective sleeping position and this sets up a conflict – as we restlessly toss and turn we are trying to return to our habitual position and are resisting the new one.

Sleeping partners

There is also evidence to suggest that body postures during sleep can reveal the state of a couple's relationship. Californian psychologist John Larner carried out an unusual experiment for three months by fixing a delayed exposure film camera to the ceiling of his bedroom. This camera was loaded with special film which carried a digitally recorded time code on each frame, and recorded the sleep positions of Larner and his wife. By day the couple kept detailed diaries which recorded their feelings for each other, as well as day-to-day events. It emerged that changes in their sleep positions could definitely be linked to daytime events.

Not surprisingly, after a bad quarrel the couple would lie far apart from each other as they settled down for the night. But since the camera was able to record the sleepers throughout the night, it was able to show the unconscious process of making up which took place. In one example, John Larner recorded in his journal that he had instigated a particular argument. That night his sleeping body began to move towards his wife's while she righteously remained on her side of the bed. He then reached out to touch her – while they both slept, apparently oblivious of their nocturnal body language. Similarly, when the couple noted feeling particularly loving and close by day they would sleep wrapped in each other's arms for about an hour before assuming another position.

Sex and sleep
Love-making also affects the sleep which follows it, for the camera recorded two or three times the usual number of body movements for a three-hour period following intercourse. Rapid eye movement (REM) sleep also increased, suggesting that more dreaming was taking place.

John Larner believed that the explanation for these higher levels of sleep activity was hormonal. 'It is quite clear that the hormonal activity generated during intense sexual love continues for some time after quiescence. The process of regenerating sperm begins immediately in the male and the whole nervous system is concentrating on that for a while. The activity in the woman's body after orgasm is complex to say the least, and there is no doubt that the more powerful the orgasm the more frantic the biological workings of both bodies become.'

How do you sleep? Read the descriptions of sleeping positions that follow and see if they provide insight into your own preferred sleeping posture.

Foetal position
This is the position of the baby when it is in the warm, dark womb and is extremely self-protective. The whole body is curled up into a ball with the knees drawn up towards the chest, the arms hugging the body.

When we sleep in the foetal position we are feeling very insecure and seeking the comfort and safety we experienced in the mother's womb before birth.

Semi-foetal

Comfortable, healthy and balanced – the semi-foetal position is among the most common of sleep positions. With knees and arms loosely bent, the sleeper can turn easily and at the same time conserve body heat, breathe properly and fully relax all muscles. Such people are not experiencing any major conflicts in their lives and are perfectly content with themselves.

Jekyll and Hyde

Resembling a stork, with one leg extended and the other bent, this position indicates a person with a dual personality. There is certainly an inner conflict between active and passive roles – such individuals may appear to be self-confident extroverts, but are secretly shy. Or perhaps the opposite is true and by presenting a non-aggressive face to the world they are concealing a far more ambitious character.

Face down

In this position the sleeper lies flat out, face down with arms and legs stretched out. By dominating the sleeping space in this way they are seeking to control their lives. It is usually very hard to move such people – awake or asleep – for they will fight hard to defend their views. Most people who prefer this position are punctual, orderly and try to counteract feelings of insecurity by regulating their lives so that few surprises disrupt their measured existence. Control is a word which has a special meaning for them.

Flat out

Secure, happy and supremely confident – these sleepers spread out and take over large amounts of space. Lying on their backs they extend their arms and legs freely and fearlessly. Such a position suggests a secure personality who is used to getting plenty of attention and is not afraid to be completely open whether awake or asleep. And there is something endearingly childlike about their trusting attitude which adds to their popularity.

WHEN YOU'RE SMILING

Someone who smiles a lot tends to have a more positive effect on others than a person who is always serious. A happy smile lights up the face, makes you look younger and attracts people to you. Indeed, not surprisingly, smilers are thought of as warm, outgoing people – while those who restrict this expression are perceived as cold and withdrawn. And since the expression of happiness in a smile is readily recognized all over the world, smiling is probably one of the most important components of body language we possess. Heartfelt smiles are unique to human beings, and recent scientific research has uncovered other reasons to be cheerful.

SMILE POWER

The expression on your face can actually dramatically alter your feelings and perceptions, and it has been proved that deliberately smiling or frowning can create corresponding emotional responses. This idea was first put forward by a French physiologist, Israel Waynbaum, in 1906. He believed that different facial expressions affected the flow of blood to the brain, and that this could create positive or negative feelings. A happy smile or irrepressible laughter increased the blood flow and contributed to joyful feelings. But sad, angry expressions decreased the flow of oxygen-carrying blood, and created a vicious circle of gloom and depression by effectively starving the brain of essential fuel.

Psychologist Robert Zajonc rediscovered this early research, and suggests that the temperature of the brain could affect the production and synthesis of neurotransmitters – which definitely influence our moods and energy levels. He argues that an impaired blood flow could not only deprive the brain of oxygen, but create further chemical imbalance through inhibiting these vital hormonal messages. Zajonc goes on to propose that our brains remember that smiling is associated with being happy, and that by deliberately smiling through your tears you can persuade your brain to release uplifting neurotransmitters – replacing a depressed condition with a happier one. People suffering from psychosomatic illness, depression and anxiety states could benefit from simply exercising their zygomatic muscles – which pull the corners of the mouth up and back to form a smile – several times an hour.

PUT ON A HAPPY FACE

'I fashion the expression of my face,
as accurately as possible,
in accordance with the expression of his,
and then wait to see what thoughts or sentiments arise in my mind
or heart.'

The Purloined Letter, Edgar Allan Poe.

Further in-depth research has been undertaken by Paul Ekman at the University of California. Ekman wanted to discover whether the autonomic nervous system is affected by different emotional expressions, so he set up an experiment in which a number of volunteers were asked to fake facial gestures associated with feelings. Concentrating on six simple emotions – fear, disgust, anger, surprise, sadness and happiness – Ekman wired up his volunteers to equipment which could register any changes in temperature, heart rate, skin resistance and muscle tension. Each expression was held for ten seconds, as participants were requested to contract various facial muscles and remember each emotion in turn.

Negative and anxious facial expressions produced very definite stress reactions in the autonomic nervous system. And anger resulted in the most dramatic changes of all, as heart rates increased and temperatures rose. Happy faces exerted a calming effect upon the body, which seemed to continue after the exercise. Of course, neither negative nor positive effects are permanent – but it does look as though people whose expressions are habitually miserable may be needlessly damaging their health.

Another experiment which adds further credence to this theory was conducted with a group of people who were asked to smile or frown for no apparent reason. They were then split into groups and shown some films, during which they were asked to monitor their feelings and prevailing mood.

Those who had been asked to frown were shown quite cheerful films, while the smiling guinea pigs were shown sad or upsetting films. Yet the participants who had been asked to frown reported feeling sad or angry even though they were watching uplifting material. And sad images failed to affect the smilers, who said they felt positive about what they had seen. The implication of these results is that it is in our power to influence our moods beneficially.

LIGHT UP YOUR FACE WITH GLADNESS

Are you frowning as you read this? Habitual frowners may not even be aware that their foreheads are creased, and will need to touch their brows to find out. A permanent frown is forbidding and unattractive, yet it is very easy to fall into the habit of frowning. You can stop yourself by placing your hand on your forehead to check whether your brow is smooth whenever you are reading or watching television. In this way you can begin to unlearn a negative piece of body language – and if you suffer from headaches, you should find yourself suffering less.

Smiling at yourself may make you feel rather self-conscious – but it works. Next time you are under the weather, physically or emotionally, you can test the therapeutic powers of smiling for yourself. Each time the expression fades from your face, try again and again until you begin to notice an improvement in yourself. In a large number of cases, this simple technique will produce noticeable benefits within a short space of time – and it's free.

Smiling at someone else can really help both of you to feel better, for a smile tends to call forth an answering smile. Paul Ekman believes that one of the reasons why we are attracted to smiling faces is because they can actually affect our autonomic nervous system. Facial expressions and moods, he says, are catching, for we are not simply registering that someone is cheerful or cross – we are experiencing the same emotion. So if you are always surrounded by miserable people with long faces, you are likely to suffer depressive feelings yourself eventually. Many experts believe that laughing and smiling are powerful adjuncts to conventional medicine. Their message is – happiness heals.

THE LANGUAGE OF SMILES

A wide variety of feelings are expressed by smiles. From broad beams of pleasure and shy smiles, to the enigmatic smile on the face of the Mona Lisa and wry lopsided grins; from polite social smiles to false smiles – this gesture reveals many nuances of emotion. Professor Paul Ekman's research has identified three main kinds of smile, each denoting a different type of emotion. The FELT SMILE, the MISERABLE SMILE and the FALSE SMILE all make different use of the facial muscles and so it becomes possible to differentiate between them with practice.

THE FELT SMILE

This smile is the genuine article, expressing spontaneous pleasure, amusement and joy. The zygomatic major muscle raises the corners of the mouth, while the orbicularis oculi lifts up the cheek and draws the skin around the eye socket inwards. The more powerful the emotion, the more defined this muscle action is. Yet even the most heartfelt smile is rarely held for longer than four seconds, and may last as briefly as two-thirds of a second.

Generally speaking, this kind of smile falls into three categories, which were defined by British researchers Christopher Brannigan and David Humphries. The simple smile occurs when the mouth turns up, but the lips remain closed – and indicates a private pleasure, for it is most often seen when people smile to themselves. The upper smile exposes the upper teeth – and is the most common smile of greeting between people, usually involving simultaneous eye contact. The broad smile exposes both sets of teeth, and usually grows broader and broader until it turns into a laugh. Eye contact rarely happens with this type of smile.

THE MISERABLE SMILE

'Seldom he smiles, and smiles in such a sort
As if he mocked himself, and scorned his spirit,
That could be moved to smile at anything.'
Julius Ceasar, William Shakespeare.

Professor Ekman's Miserable Smile occurs when someone is acknowledging defeat or unhappiness, and is usually performed in front of others. Lopsided, wry smiles signal both distress and our resignation to the quirks of cruel fate. Indeed, they are characterized by their asymmetrical shape – as if half the mouth were smiling, and the other half sunk in misery.

THE FALSE SMILE

'O villain, villain, smiling, damned villain!
My tables, – meet it is I set it down,
That one may smile, and smile, and be a villain. . .'
Hamlet, William Shakespeare.

A False Smile is also more asymmetrical than a genuine smile, and is deliberately misleading. In addition, it lasts longer than the real variety, and is slower to spread across the face. The fixed professional smiles of insincere salesmen, actors and other people who have to smile in their jobs are all examples of the false smile in operation. In Japan, however, it is polite to smile when you don't mean it. Even when upset, the Japanese will don what is effectively a social mask required by their society. One recent experiment in Japan involved a group of Japanese who were shown some very disturbing medical films. A hidden camera recorded individual reactions of fear, disgust and distress on the viewers' faces. But when an authority figure, in the person of a white-coated scientist, entered the room they concealed their negative emotions in his presence by smiling.

How can you recognise a false smile? The biggest giveaway is the eyes, which narrow and crinkle up when the smile comes from the heart – and remain unaffected when someone is covering up negative emotions. So, first check the eyes for smile lines, and warmth of expression – then look closely at the mouth. The upper lip will be raised in an exaggerated way, while the lower lip appears to be squared without any movement in the jaw. When people are forced to smile for a photographer, they will often produce a false smile, especially if they don't really want to have their picture taken in the first place.

Dr. Ewan Grant of Birmingham University describes another fake smile, which he calls the 'oblong smile'. This accurately describes the shape made by the mouth when the lips are drawn back fully from the teeth into a kind of polite grimace. The oblong smile may be seen when someone is pretending to be amused, or when people find themselves in an awkward social situation – such as receiving unwanted sexual attention – and do not know how to extricate themselves. By pretending to smile they are buying time, and hoping to placate whoever is causing their sense of unease.

Yet most people can detect the conflict between an apparently cheerful facial expression and what is lurking beneath. The old idea that you should try to look happy and bright when delivering bad news simply doesn't work, for psychologists have found that in such instances people ignore body language and concentrate on what is being said.

A false smile rarely deceives anyone for long, for it produces an uncomfortable sensation in the onlooker – who may not be able to analyze his or her reaction to it, but instinctively knows something's not quite right. The muscles around our eyes which we use when really smiling cannot be brought under conscious control by the brain – so in this case it is only the lips which can lie.

THE LANGUAGE OF LAUGHTER

The most wasted of all days is that on which one has not laughed.

Maxims et pensées, Nicolas Chamfort.

Fifteen facial muscles contract in a co-ordinated reflex action, breathing changes, and up to twelve separate gestures are performed when we laugh. Cackling like parrots, or braying like donkeys, our laughter ranges from a brief snigger to completely uncontrollable belly-laughter where we heave, shed tears, and rock about helplessly. So what is laughter, and why do we laugh?

Ritual threat

'But Lord! to see the absurd nature of Englishmen that cannot forbear laughing and jeering at everything that looks strange.'

Samuel Pepys

The noted ethologist, Professor Eibl-Eibesfeldt, suggests that the innate response of laughter is a form of ritualized threat. Numerous other animals will form themselves into a group to threaten other hostile animals. And monkeys, for example, bare their teeth and make a rhythmic sound akin to laughter when they are displaying aggression. People, says Eibl-Eibesfeldt, laugh at others or about others and enjoy doing this in groups. The object of derision experiences laughter as aggressive, but the audience or laughing group feel a mutual bond through this shared activity.

This aspect of humour is always prominent during times of war, when cartoonists, comedians and wits do their best to ridicule the enemy and raise spirits. School-children often invent jokes about their teachers – particularly the more forbidding ones.

Freud considered hostile humour provided a safety-valve in situations where open aggression would be impossible or inappropriate. 'By making an enemy small, inferior, despicable or comic,' he writes, 'we achieve in a roundabout way the enjoyment of overcoming him.'

So-called 'blue' jokes are hostile in another way, for according to Freud they are acts of sexual aggression resulting from repression. Hidden attitudes and fears may be safely revealed in a humorous way which might otherwise embarrass us. Next time you are with a group of people, and one of them tells an obscene joke you will be able to discern how embarrassed various individuals are by watching how they laugh. Feeling ashamed and amused at the same time creates a conflict, and anyone in this predicament will put hand over mouth in a subconscious attempt to hide or stifle laughter. And although we have come a long way since prudish Victorians clothed their 'obscene' table legs, we have an equally long way to go before sex ceases to cause controversy.

Frightfully jolly

Other anthropologists, including Dr. Desmond Morris, argue that laughter is a response which is very close to tears. Photographs of laughing faces are sometimes almost impossible to distinguish from pictures of people howling with grief, and of course hysterical laughter can easily turn to tears. Playing hide-and-seek games, and pulling funny faces at young children produces dual sensations of alarm and delight – which in turn result in a combination of crying and gurgling. It is this combination which we call laughter, and in young children it can easily end in tears, for fearful instincts are still very strong.

Proponents of this theory maintain that we laugh when something is strange or shocking, but ultimately non-threatening to our well-being. And horror-film audiences do sometimes laugh in a relieved way, usually when they have been frightened enough and realize that, after all, it is only a film. We also respond to shock by laughing – again with relief. Indeed, lunches or teas after funerals are often noticeably filled with laughing guests who are perhaps reassuring themselves of their own vitality in the face of death.

TICKLING

Are you ticklish? And why should tickling make you laugh? These questions have puzzled many scientists, and possible explanations would seem to indicate that tickling is a form of mock-attack – to which we respond with laughter. The tantalising build-up of tension which accompanies such games as 'This Little Piggy' or 'Round and Round the Garden, Like a Teddy Bear' finds release when the tickling finally begins, and we can laugh freely. And the usual sites for a tickling attack, such as the soles of the feet or under the arms, are richly supplied with a high density of protective nerve-endings. These areas are, therefore, particularly sensitive to attack and laughter indicates that we realise the attack is only in fun.

Many adults seem to become less ticklish as they grow older, but no-one is certain why this should be so. Possibly the answer is psychological, for we perceive adulthood as a serious time and tend to regard those who laugh a lot as inconsequential or stupid. It seems we cannot take jovial people seriously, perhaps because certain forms of mental disturbance are characterized by pointless baying laughter, which hints at a vacant mind.

LAUGH AND BE WELL

Considerable research has now been done into the physiology of laughing. And the results bear out the old maxim that laughter is the best medicine. When we laugh, every organ in the body is affected in such a positive way that it has been called 'stationary jogging'. Our breathing quickens as we inhale deeply and exhale through our vocal chords. This exercises the face, neck and shoulders, stomach and diaphragm. In addition blood pressure is reduced, while blood vessels expand close to the skin's surface and improve circulation. People often seem to blush when they are laughing heartily, and this is why. Laughter also increases the amount of oxygen in the blood which helps the body to heal itself, and resist further infection. Furthermore, laughter can lower the heart rate, stimulate the appetite and burn up calories. A good laugh will also stimulate the body's natural pain-killing tranquillisers, beta-endorphins, leading some experts to suggest that laughing can prevent ulcers and digestive disorders.

MERRY MEDICINE

A French neurologist, Henri Rubinstein, has studied laughter extensively. And one of his conclusions is that just one minute of laughter provides up to forty-five minutes of subsequent relaxation. Because our muscles are relaxed, and our whole system benefits from this inborn response, many doctors now believe that laughter plays a major part in successful convalescence.

The story of American journalist Norman Cousins who cured

himself of an incurable disease is one example of just how positive this compound gesture can be. In 1964, Norman Cousins contracted a crippling inflammatory disease called ankylosing spondylitis. Physicians informed him that this condition would slowly cause his spine to seize up, so that in the end he would be unable to move. Unfortunately, they said, there was no cure for this painful and distressing illness – but they would try to make him comfortable in hospital.

At first, he was understandably miserable and depressed by the diagnosis. But Cousins decided to fight back, and declining painkillers he discharged himself from the hospital and booked into an hotel. There he hired numerous comedy films, and had a nurse read to him from humorous books. He discovered that ten minutes of helpless laughter could create pain-free intervals of two hours or more. And medical tests taken before and after these sessions showed that they were having a measurably healing effect upon his illness. His months of struggling to cure the incurable paid off, and he was able to return to full-time work. And more than twenty years later he is still delivering lectures about his experiences. Laughter had performed a miracle.

A NATURAL HIGH

Dr. Vernon Coleman endorses the idea that laughter can help us to help ourselves. In his book, *Mind Power*, he writes: 'When I worked as a hospital doctor we always used to have a Christmas pantomime for the younger patients. And the number of painkillers that we had to dish out on the day of the pantomime was always very low. Laughter isn't just a pleasant experience. It is a positive, natural phenomenon which helps to ensure that the body benefits to the fullest extent. It may well be that laughter really is the best medicine!'

He goes on to suggest that we try to surround ourselves with happy people, because smiles and laughter are contagious. Making an effort not to take ourselves too seriously is also an important factor, for an ability to laugh at yourself can provide rapid relief from tension – and help to put things in perspective. And following Norman Cousins's example, you can also collect funny books – or obtain copies of films which really make you laugh. Every time you feel low, you can use this comedy store to change both your perceptions and your body chemistry. For whether aggression or alarm – or a mixture of both – are the origins of this innate response, we can only benefit from letting more of it into our lives. Have you performed this particular compound gesture today?

THE LANGUAGE OF TEARS

The ability to weep is yet another uniquely human form of emotional response. Some scientists have suggested that human tears are evidence of an aquatic past – but this does not seem very likely. We cry from the moment we enter this world, for a number of reasons. Helpless babies cry to alert their parents because they are ill, hungry or uncomfortable. As they develop they will also cry just to attract parental attention, and will often stop when they get it. As we get older, and learn to laugh, we seem to cry less often unless very upset, or when a helpless fit of laughter leads to tears.

The idea that having a good cry can do you good is a very old one. And now it has scientific validity, for recent research into tears has shown that tears contain a natural painkiller called enkaphalin. This chemical helps you to feel better by fighting sorrow and pain – and weeping can increase the quantities of ankaphalin you produce, and free you from pent-up emotions. When someone has had a shock, is very stressed, or in a lot of pain the natural response is to cry.

Unfortunately, in our society we place restrictions upon this naturally healing activity. Boys, in particular, are admonished when they cry – for it is still regarded by some people as a sign of masculine weakness. This kind of repression can only increase stress, both emotionally and physically.

Tears of emotion also help the body rid itself of toxic chemical wastes, for they have been found to contain more protein than tears which result from cold winds or other irritants. If no tears are shed because they are being repressed, these wastes remain in the body.Crying comforts, calms, and can be very enjoyable – witness the popularity of the highly emotional films which have been dubbed 'weepies'. It seems that people enjoy crying together almost as much as laughing together.

THE LANGUAGE OF FRIENDSHIP

Friendship adds breadth and colour to our lives. And like all our relationships, friends and acquaintances require understanding if our association with them is to develop and deepen with time. Use and knowledge of body language can enrich your social life – by providing valuable insights into others' personalities, and enabling you to transmit the kind of friendly signals which can improve your chances of making new friends.

FIRST IMPRESSIONS
The importance of body language during the first four to five minutes of an encounter cannot be over-emphasized, for while we are engaged in making small talk we are forming a lasting impression of each other. And although this impression is formed quickly it is a lingering one, which can radically affect the outcome of an encounter. So what do we look at or absorb when we first meet somebody?

Firstly, we assess physical appearance, which will furnish information about age, sex, perceived status and attractiveness. And depending upon what we see, we will react accordingly. For example, most people will behave more politely if they think someone holds a position in life superior to their own. In time gone by elderly people were automatically accorded higher status, and respected for their wisdom. Remnants of ancestor worship in various ancient cultures bear witness to this particular kind of behaviour, which is now almost extinct in Western society as a whole. Status today depends very much on worldly power, and material belongings – indeed, whole industries cater to mankind's need for so-called 'status symbols' which silently signal an individual's success.

Sexual identity is another area which has altered somewhat with time. Yet we still find men or women masquerading as their opposite numbers disturbing. This is partly because we do respond differently to people of the opposite sex, and any uncertainty as to their true identity confuses our innate reactions.

But deciding whether someone is attractive is not just a

55

gender-orientated decision. Everyone enjoys looking at someone who is physically appealing, and this is not simply a question of sexual attraction – for heterosexual men and women make such judgements every day about their own sex.

While we are looking, we are also listening – and gathering further information from the voice. No-one really pays much attention to the trivial exchanges which take place when we first meet somebody – but we do pay attention to the sound of small talk. The tone, volume, pitch and quality of a voice tells us about someone's probable age, sex, nationality, and levels of confidence. And phrases such as 'I don't like the sound of this' are based upon our underlying ability to analyse the sound rather than the content of a conversation.

Posture, gesture, touch and the ever-changing world of facial expression complete this rapid portrait of a stranger. A fuller, factual picture will be built up during later conversation – but body language provides the foundation upon which friendship is built. Your initial reaction may be altered for better or worse in the future; however, it is filed away in your memory bank and may be difficult to change consciously.

HERE'S LOOKING AT YOU

Whether or not you like the look of someone has a lot to do with how they look at you, for eye contact speaks visual volumes. During a friendly conversation people look at one another frequently, but for short periods of time. Only lovers, or would-be lovers, extend eye contact as they helplessly gaze into each other's eyes. A less pleasant form of lengthy staring occurs when one person seeks to dominate or threaten another.

Minimal mutual eye contact, however, is to be avoided – because it suggests submission, bad manners and dishonesty. Many painfully shy individuals suffer from an inability to look others in the eye, and are often wrongly assumed to be unpleasant characters as a result. Sorrow and depression are also states of mind which affect our eye language considerably.

With practice, it should be possible to determine what people are discussing by closely observing their gaze behaviour. When general conversation is taking place, people will glance at each other two-thirds of the time, looking at each other simultaneously for only a second or less. And the listener will be spending 75 per cent of the time looking, while the speaker will glance at his or her audience for only 40 per cent of talking time. Everyone looks more while they are listening – especially if extrovert, or female. Quiet, thoughtful introverts and men seem to look less often.

People who are already close friends, or who like each other, look more often than strangers. Yet even intimate friends will reduce eye contact when they are talking about very personal feelings, or potentially embarrassing topics. Since talking about intimate subjects can make us feel extremely uncomfortable, reducing mutual gaze helps diminish stress and creates an illusion of privacy.

Studies have shown that we also use eye contact to regulate conversations. When people are speaking for any length of time, they will engage in normal levels of eye contact – but as they are coming to the end of their speech, they will gaze steadily at their listener. The listener responds to this signal by glancing away, and beginning to talk. Conscious awareness of this sign can improve your conversations, by promoting better timing.

FACE TO FACE

'Your face, my thane, is as a book where men
May read strange matters.'

Macbeth, William Shakespeare.

Facial expressions, and micro-expressions, are constantly changing in response to inner and outer stimuli. And when we look at someone's face we are quickly able to tell whether the person is interested, bored, cheerful or downcast. In turn, we consciously or unconsciously use our own facial signals to convey a wide range of emotions and emphasize what we are saying.

Different sets of muscles, and parts of the face, are used to show various emotions. Shock and surprise are revealed by raised eyebrows and widened eyes, and are usually accompanied by a gasping, or open mouth. Fear and sadness, two of the most difficult emotions to fake, are registered in the eyes. Anger prevades the whole face with hostile force, while happiness seems to act like a temporary face-lift, lightening and lifting the lips and cheeks. Generally speaking, a mobile, expressive face is perceived as belonging to a more interesting, warm personality than an inscrutably static face.

HEAD IN THE RIGHT DIRECTION

Whenever you are talking or listening, even on the telephone, your head is busily moving up and down and side to side – as if engaged in a complicated ritual dance. And every nod, shake, tilt and toss synchronizes both with what is being said and what is being felt. When we are talking, we use our heads in the same way as our hands – to add weight and drama to what we're saying. This type of body language is more often used by men, who seem to nod more than women when they are speaking.

Sometimes, of course, the verbal message may directly contradict what someone genuinely feels or believes – in which case a careful observation of head movements will reveal the truth sooner or later. People unconsciously shake their heads when they are making a statement with which they disagree, or when they feel uncertain – and when this gesture is backed up by other signs of confusion, you may be sure that you cannot believe everything you are hearing.

Nodding your head is often such an automatic thing to do that you are probably unaware of it most of the time. Yet this simple gesture can actually affect the length and content of a conversation. For we don't just nod our heads when we mean yes, we also use this movement to encourage the other person by demonstrating our attention and approval of what is being said. Tilting the head to one side is another sign we use to indicate attentiveness – and is a recognizably feminine gesture, rarely employed by men. This may partly explain why women have a better reputation as good listeners.

But without these wordless conversational aids, discussions tend to become stilted and short-lived, for it is as if the speaker is talking into a void. Should you wish to use body language to bring an encounter to an abrupt close, just reduce eye contact to a minimum and keep your head still – your companion will soon fall into an uncomfortable silence.

THE SOUND OF YOUR VOICE

No two people sound exactly alike, and the sound of your voice is an important part of your personality. Its sound, richness of tone, pitch and accent relay a great deal of information about you to anyone who hears it – even when they can't see you. Some voices are so seductive that they increase our attention to that person –

while others are so dreary and monotonous that we find it difficult to pay attention to what is being said. The ancient Latin word 'persona' itself has two meanings – it describes a theatrical mask which actors wore to show the audience what type of character they were portraying. But split the word in two and you have 'per sona', which means 'by sound'. So an individual is not just judged by the face he or she presents to the world, but also by the sound he or she makes.

Yet few people can realistically assess their own sound, and are often shocked when they hear it on tape. The non-verbal content of speech is an important, and frequently overlooked, part of our body language. Research in the field of paralinguistics has revealed that the actual sound of speech influences 38 per cent of every meeting. The study of paralinguistics examines all nonverbal aspects of speech, including volume, speed of speaking, pitch, tone and speech errors – such as stammering.

The unique sound which broadcasts your vocal characteristics to the world is physically created by three elements. A flow of pressurized air acts on the vocal chords to produce vibration, the vocal chords themselves acting as vibratory instruments, then this sound is magnified by resonating cavities in the head. How you breathe affects voice projection too – when you are tense, for example, your diaphragm may tense up and distort the quality of your voice, producing unexpected changes in volume and pitch. And the familiar sensation of butterflies in the stomach indicates an equally fluttery diaphragm, which will cause the voice to shake. Feelings of severe strain reveal themselves in a hoarse, strained voice – for acute tension in the neck and throat muscles affect vocal resonance. Different emotions are expressed through their own characteristic sounds – anger sharpens the voice and increases its volume, we scream in terror, and sorrow lowers and distorts the voice with sobs.

SUCCESSFUL SPEECH

Try to sound confident and positive. Thin, weak voices seem to lack vital energy and do not inspire confidence in others. Do you speak loudly, or softly? Quiet voices project a submissive image, and were often admired in women for this reason. But avoid extremes – turning up the volume suggests dominance and aggression, neither of which are qualities generally sought in a friendship. Neither should you pitch your voice too high – women especially should be wary of sounding like superannuated three-year-olds. Avoid gabbling, for nobody trusts a fast talker.

You can easily enliven your speech by stressing positive words and phrases, and subtly altering the pitch and volume when you wish to emphasize a dramatic point. Actors and other public speakers make expressive use of their voices when delivering speeches, and you can learn some of their tricks quite easily. In addition, listening to your own voice on a tape recorder can be a great help, enabling you to pinpoint any faults you may have.

POSTURE, GESTURE AND TOUCH

Posture, gesture and touch are vital ingredients of every encounter. Our facial expressions, voice and eye language communicate our emotions, while posture indicates our strength of feeling and underlying mood. Three prominent experts in the field of body language have established various categories of gesture, many of which appear in mixed clusters as the conversation progresses.

GESTURE CLUSTERS

Paul Ekman and Wallace Friesen suggest the following:

- **emblems**: gestures which are substitutes for words, such as sign-language;
- **illustrators**: emphatic, expansive movements which amplify the spoken word, 'it was this big', 'he's not very tall' for example;
- **regulators**: nonverbal ways of indicating whether we wish to speak, or listen, or want to change our role during a conversation;
- **adaptors**: displacement activities, and other gestures which reveal emotional reactions;
- **displays**: obvious gestures displaying emotion, such as clenching an angry fist, or sinking head into hands in despair.

Michael Argyle indicates five slightly different divisions:

- **illustrations,** and body language directly linked to speech;
- **conventional signs and sign language,** such as deaf and dumb mime, or ticktack signals which are used on racecourses;
- **emotional gestures;**
- **movements indicative of character,** including the use of open and closed body language;
- **ritual gestures,** such as those used in religious contexts.

You and your shadow

Postural and gestural echoing is a fascinating area of body language, which has been observed all over the world. Since friendship is an alliance of equals, we like to share with our friends, and by copying their postures and gestures our body language confirms that we are thinking and feeling like the other person. However, it is usually an unconscious form of behaviour, which can only be recognized with hindsight. Any social occasion will provide you with an opportunity to observe sympathetic mimicry in action – sometimes people will even cross their legs in unison, or lean forward at the same moment as if they were literally of one mind.

Next time you find yourself talking to someone you find unsympathetic or withdrawn, you could try this experiment for yourself by adopting the other's body language and some of his or her more frequent gestures. If this is done subtly, you may find your companion talking more freely to you than before.

Mirror, mirror

Further research into the synchrony of body language has shown that when two people have established a lasting friendship, their tiniest, most fleeting physical expressions mirror each other. Slow-motion film has revealed this mysterious rhythm which can be seen in passing facial expressions, brief nods and jerks of the head, and even in the tensing and relaxing of the fingers.

Postural and gestural echoing also synchronizes with conversational rhythms in an extraordinary way. At the beginning of a discussion the listener begins to echo the body language of the speaker, including the actual speed of speech, by making silent answering tilts and jerks of his own body. Often these movements are so subtle that they can only be revealed by slow-motion film. The listener will then usually reduce the amount of movement he is making, and absorb the content of what is being said until he is ready to make a reply. At this point, there is an increase in movement once again but this time the body language no longer echoes that of the speaker – although the rhythm remains the same. This kind of movement is one of several signals we use to convey a desire to speak. Therefore, this is yet another instance where attention to body language can significantly improve your ability to communicate with other people.

HAND SIGNALS – A USER'S GUIDE

- **clenched hands:** when speaking, clenched hands indicate that what is being talked about is frustrating, or was a painful experience. When listening it tells you that the listener is responding negatively.
- **steepling:** the fingertips and thumbs are pressed together, forming a triangular shape – which is then held up near the face, at waist level, or in the lap. This signals confidence or certainty of opinion. If the head is tilted back at the same time, it suggests arrogance.
- **hands clasped lightly behind the back:** a supremely confident gesture, laying the whole, vulnerable front of the body theoretically open to attack. Frequently used by royalty.
- **arms folded with thumbs pointing upwards:** a message combining defensiveness and superiority. You will find it nearly impossible to convince the other person of anything, for the mind is resolutely closed. You could try handing him or her a cup of coffee.
- **hand resting lightly on the cheek:** your audience is analyzing and evaluating what you are saying before making a decision.
- **head resting on, or being supported by, the hand:** at best your listener is very tired, at worst you are boring him or her.
- **hand stroking or rubbing the chin:** again, your ideas are being given careful consideration.
- **hand clasping the back of the neck:** danger signal; this person is trying to control angry feelings which cannot be expressed openly.
- **both hands behind the head:** another sign of superiority, confidence, and possibly arrogance.
- **lightly scratching or rubbing the side of the neck with one or two fingers:** your audience may think you are lying, your ideas may be unfamiliar or controversial, or the situation creates insecurity.
- **scratching the head:** perplexity, doubt and uncertainty.
- **hiding the thumbs inside the fist:** difficulty in analyzing a problem.
- **using the index finger to point at another person, or group:** dominance, authoritarianism, aggression.
- **clenched fists:** not to be confused with passively clenched hands. Clenched fists are often moved about during speech and are undeniably aggressive and threatening.
- **rubbing the hands together:** quick rubbing indicates a pleasurable sense of satisfaction or expectation, while slow rubbing or wringing of the hands reveals that a 'con' is about to be perpetrated.
- **separating the little finger from the rest of the fingers:** shows possible eccentricity and strong sense of individuality.
- **hands pressed together, as if in prayer:** demonstrates a desire to persuade, or underline a point gently but firmly.

THE TELL-TALE TOUCH

Your whole body is covered with a sensitive sensory organ – your skin, which constantly relays messages to the brain. And it has been performing this function for you since before you were born. Touch tells us a great deal about our environment, ourselves, and other people. It is so essential for our health and happiness that babies deprived of it rapidly sicken, and may even die. Indeed, when people feel insecure they often touch themselves by wrapping their arms around their shoulders or torso – as if giving themselves a reassuring hug.

This kind of self-touching also serves to affirm our solidity, our boundaries, and our reality. One of the reasons people feel better on a typical seaside holiday is because their skin is exposed to the heat of the sun, the movement of air and water, and is being massaged with creams and oils several times a day. For most of the year the average skin leads a lonely existence – hidden under clothes, touched only in a sexual or professional context, and more or less ignored the rest of the time. Yet we are all profoundly influenced by it, as the following interesting experiment clearly demonstrates.

A university library assistant was asked to touch the hands of some students when returning their library cards. Other students are not touched, although the librarian's behaviour did not vary in any other way. The students were then asked to say what they thought of the library, and the library assistant. All the people who had been touched felt more positive about the library and the assistant, than those who had not. Significantly, even those students who didn't recall the assistant's brief physical contact with them were affected. Other research, conducted in California, indicates that tactile people tend to be more attractive than non-touchers.

But as with all body language, a consideration of culture, character and context is vital if your message is not to be misunderstood. If somebody is radiating hostile or defensive vibrations, hugging them in a loving way is unlikely to help change their mood – it may even worsen matters by seeming invasive and threatening. Far better to start slowly with a brief squeeze of the hand, or a fleeting touch on the shoulder – both relatively neutral areas. As they gradually calm down, you can move in closer without upsetting them.

Touch types

The language of touch falls into the following five basic categories:

- **professional touch**: into this category comes the touch of medical practitioners, teachers, and beauty therapists of every kind. Being touched by these people can be experienced as soothing – in the case of a massage for example, or frightening – medical and dental examinations are often highly stressful events.
- **social touch**: about 60 per cent of all greetings and farewells include the element of touch as part of the ritual. And, as we shall see later, a polite handshake can be very revealing.
- **friendly touch**: this ranges from a passing pat on the forearm when making a point, to the enthusiastic embraces of footballers on a winning streak. It denotes warmth, encouragement, sympathy and occasionally dominance on the part of the toucher. You are more likely to enjoy touching, and being touched, if it was part of your family background. People who grow up in non-tactile families have mixed feelings about touch in adult life, and need to feel very secure with someone before they can accept even the most fleeting contact.
- **loving touch**: lovers, parent and child, very close friends all touch each other in more intimate ways than casual aquaintances. And these ways demonstrate the degree of trust present in the relationship – although again it varies from one culture to another.
- **sexual touch**: which gives sensual pleasure leading to sexual arousal and love-making.

WHEN DO WE TOUCH?

You are more likely to touch and be touched in specific circumstances – the most obvious being when saying hello and goodbye, or when making love. But other emotions and intentions have been shown to increase the incidence of touch between people. Touch is more likely

- when telling someone what to do
- when asking a favour
- when sympathizing with someone
- when attempting to persuade someone
- when giving advice
- when happy and excited about something that's happened to you
- in your social life, rather than at work

SAYING HELLO

'Anyone who sought to list all the different national forms of greeting could easily fill a book with them... One would be confronted by enormous variety, one would come across apparently more or less inexplicable peculiarities, and one would be left amazed at the subtly cultivated etiquette of forms of greeting.'

Ethnographische Parallelen und Vergleiche   R. Andrée.

Books, films and television have – to a certain extent – standardized our body language, especially in the Western world. Yet diversity still manifests itself – personality, relationship and status all affect the way we greet one another, and the intensity of emotion we display each time.

Primitive and tribal people still evince an astonishing variety of greetings, including the most widespread form of social salutation – the handshake. Extending a hand to encourage and reassure another is something we all have in common with chimpanzees. Dominant chimps hold out their hands to lower-ranking members of their tribe, who will often beg for such contact – for it gives them courage and strength.

Another, probably innate, greeting phenomenon is the eyebrow flash – which has been observed by anthropologists all over the world. This friendly signal occurs spontaneously as we make visual contact with someone we know, and seems to be body shorthand for pleased surprise. The eyebrows are raised for a fraction of a second, usually accompanied by a welcoming smile.

What a handshake can say

'There is a hand that has not heart in it, there is a claw or paw, a flipper or fin, a bit of wet cloth to take hold of, a piece of unbaked dough, a cold clammy thing we recoil from, or greedy clutch with the heat of sin, which we drop as a burning coal.'

The Rising Faith, C.A. Bartol.

A dominant farmer and a shy city-dweller shake hands in very different ways – for a handshake is similar to a signature, in that it is an integral part of the personality. Of course, by modifying your handshake, you can improve your initial image – always remembering the lasting impact of the first four to five minutes of an encounter. Basically, a firm positive handshake produces the best results for it inspires confidence. The purpose of a handshake is to create a momentary physical bond between people, which says 'hello' or 'goodbye' or 'we agree on this'.

Weak, limp handshakes transmit such a half-hearted message that they tend to undermine an otherwise positive situation. Clearly, this does not apply to visiting royalty – or anyone else who has to shake many people by the hand as part of a ceremony or social event. A limp hand is then highly recommended as a means of avoiding fatigue. Certain forms of illness also weaken the body, resulting in an ineffectual grip. Subsequent body signals must always be considered, but they become particularly important under such circumstances.

Who's on top?

A handshake can be a symbolic power struggle between two dominant individuals. It can signal mutual respect, or it can tell you – quite literally – who's on top of the situation.

A dominant hand will automatically face palm down when clasping the other person's hand, so that their palm faces upwards. Open, outward facing palms denote submission and are non-threatening. So by initiating this type of handshake, the dominant individual immediately places the less aggressive partner in a submissive position.

Two aggressive individuals shaking hands will therefore create a firm, vertical handshake verging on the vice-like as they both unconsciously seek to gain the upper hand. Recognizing one another's strong characters these two should eventually establish mutual respect, and a potentially balanced partnership.

Best foot forward

Australian management consultant Allan Pease has done considerable research into handshakes, and suggests that the following technique may be an effective way of diffusing a dominant handshake – and gaining control of the situation. As you extend your hand in greeting, step forward with your left foot. Now bringing your right foot across, move to the left in front of the other person. You have now invaded his personal space, and as you complete the movement by bringing the left leg across to your right leg you can easily turn the handshake into an equal, vertical one. These manoeuvres may take some practice, for not many people are naturally left-footed. But by stepping automatically into a handshake with your left foot you can at least begin an association on equal footing.

Town and country

Personal space requirements also affect our greeting behaviour, because of regional and cultural variations. Country dwellers have a larger intimate zone than people living in cities, and will stand further away from you when shaking hands. The arm will extend to its full length too, in order to demonstrate the size of their private territory.

Someone who was either brought up in a town, or who has become used to living in one, will move in much closer and the distance between wrist and body will be markedly smaller. Recognizing these basic differences when first meeting people should help you modify your own body language, so that you avoid unwittingly threatening others – or seeming cold and distant. And don't forget to smile as if you mean it, for this is the single most disarming piece of body language we can employ.

Kissing, cuddling and stroking

Social kissing has once again become both acceptable and fashionable among younger people. Mediterranean and Russian people have always greeted each other with a kiss, irrespective of gender – but for many years only female friends kissed each other hello and goodbye. English and American men still rarely kiss, except on the sports field, but between opposite-sex friends the custom has become so widespread that handshaking has been relegated to formal events, work situations, and men only contacts. Indeed, between themselves, women have never really adopted the handshake at all. They prefer to clasp each other's hands, kiss one another on the cheek, or embrace their friends.

Dominant characters are harder to spot once body language becomes more intimate, but generally speaking the more dominant individual will make the first move when initiating touch. Even when someone opens their arms in welcome they can still relay a dominant message by standing their ground and waiting for you to come to them – rather like the head of a tribe.

Let me entertain you

If you are entertaining at home it is important to make an effort to put your guests at their ease, and one of the simplest ways of doing this is to try and meet them at the edge of what is, after all, your territory. The garden gate may be impractical, especially on dark winter evenings, but how you greet people at the front door can help to begin a meeting on the right note.

Close embraces can make people unused to them feel awkward, so reserve these for friends who expect and enjoy them. When it is difficult, or inappropriate, to touch someone you can always do it verbally. Spoken stroking includes mild flattery, telling someone how pleased you are to see them, and taking an interest in their well-being while they are under your roof.

Many traditional farewells also include an element of mutual verbal caress. 'Thank you for having me', 'Thank you for coming', and 'Take care of yourself' are modern equivalents of this ritual exchange, which further endorse the friendly body language we must all use if we wish to keep our associations in good repair.

THE TANGLED WEB

Why do we lie? There are many shades of grey between the socially expedient little white lie and the completely untrue falsehood. Indeed, in certain situations, everyone enjoys being deceived – for actors, conjurors and magicians are all lying to their audiences. And the enduring popularity of spy thrillers and whodunit novels is partly based upon our pleasure in being kept guessing, albeit in a harmless way.

A more sinister fascination with falsehood is revealed by public interest in real espionage or murder trials, where the guilt or innocence of the defendant is in doubt. Of course, most people would like to see justice done, but are equally interested in unravelling the threads of deception and intrigue running through the case.

THE CUSHIONING LIE

Social lies and less-than-sincere flattery also seem to be necessary to maintain harmony, friendships, and jobs. The phrase, 'let's have lunch sometime', is a well-known social lie which, while apparently offering a friendly meeting, rarely results in such an encounter. Yet it serves a useful purpose by enabling two people to co-operate in a harmless lie, and remain acquaintances – if not genuine friends.

Similarly, complimenting someone on his or her cooking or appearance – when both might be dreadful – allows everyone to sustain a reasonably civilised social front and avoid obvious conflict. Politicians are often adept liars, not necessarily from a desire to deceive, but from loyalty to their party's policies and leader, from ambition to be elected, or from a need to conceal sensitive information from the public.

It's important to consider all the options and motivations if you decide someone is lying to you. Apparently, it is easier to detect lies when the liar is of the opposite sex. But the surest indicator is instinct. Women make better human lie detectors than men, perhaps because they are encouraged to rely on intuition and emotional gut reactions. They are also more expressive exponents of body language – and so more practised at interpreting it. Men are often wary of what has been called 'feminine intuition'.

BEHIND THE LIE

The reasons for lying can be broken down into the following general categories:

- EXPEDIENCE: The social lie, including harmless flattery, loyalty and belief.
- NECESSITY: The professional lie, used in acting and entertainment, espionage, the law and selling.
- WITHHOLDING: Playing for time in situations where you need to evaluate the facts before committing yourself. Suppressing negative or hostile reactions to maintain the status quo.
- FEAR: Where telling the truth could result in punishment – for instance, if crime has been committed; fears of losing love, friendship or employment might also prompt a lie.
- DEFENCE: Unwillingness to admit to faults in yourself, or in someone you love.
- CRIME: Confidence tricksters are practised deceivers, and the best are pathological liars because they believe what they are saying.

LIE DETECTORS

Studies show that body language is most likely to reveal deception when the need to lie is very strong, but the liar's belief in the falsehood and confidence that it will be accepted is low. The inevitable conflict and tension that this produces will, like truth itself, get out one way or another. Autonomic signals – such as sweating, paling and altered breathing patterns are the most reliable pointers, because it is impossible to fake something like sweating – unless you happen to be an advanced yogi with complete control over your bodily functions.

These and other stress reactions result from the heightened sense of fear which lying produces. But only dramatic circumstances will cause such obvious stress symptoms to be visible to the naked eye. These autonomic reactions are measured by lie detectors, or polygraph machines, that monitor subtle changes in heart rate, skin resistance and breathing. The theory is that when someone is lying these uncontrollable reactions will give them away. Yet despite the widespread use of the polygraph in the U.S.A. both by the police, and personnel departments of large companies, its reliability is questionable. This is because individual response to circumstances varies, and some people find the situation itself so stressful that they react like liars anyway.

HOW TO SPOT A LIAR

In order to lie successfully it is essential to have control over your body language. It is easiest to lie on the telephone, or by letter, and get away with it. But while the mind may want or need to lie, and be capable of inventing a believable story, the body rarely goes along with this and will betray the mind in various ways. These signals can be broken down into categories ranging from those transmitted by the nervous system, which are the hardest to control and therefore the most truthful, to facial expressions which can be manipulated by the mind more easily.

The nervous system

As we have seen, stress signals – produced by the body's autonomic nervous system – are considered to be among the most reliable indicators of insincerity. A dry mouth, produced by fear, will cause the liar to lick his or her lips more often – and perhaps swallow nervously. There may be more throat-clearing than usual too. Breathing may become more uneven – another stress reaction which is easily observed.

However, even these signals can be misleading. Imagine an argument between two lovers – one is wrongly convinced that the other has been unfaithful. The accused person may work himself or herself up into such a frenzy while trying to convince the other of the truth, that all the classic symptoms of someone who is telling a dramatic lie will be exhibited.

Feet and legs

Your legs and feet are the most difficult parts of your body to control consciously. You can easily prove this to yourself by lying face down on the floor, stretching your legs out behind you and pointing your feet. Now try to make circles to left and right with each foot in turn, and you will realise how much mental effort you have to make to succeed.

In one study a group of people was asked to decide whether someone was lying. Half the group could see the whole body, while the others were restricted to sight of the head and face. The latter group was much more easily deceived than the group able to see the whole body, and its truthful non-verbal clues. Some organizations make a potential employee sit where the whole body is visible to the interviewer, partly because it is easier to detect unease and untruths when you can literally see the whole picture. And the farther away from the face you go, the nearer you are likely to get to the truth.

When someone chooses to lie during a conversation, he or she will often suddenly cross arms or legs simultaneously. It suggests advance self-defence against challenge. And tell-tale foot signals may include feet pointing towards the exit – revealing a desire to escape the situation – or a lot of foot tapping or jabbing movements in the air, meaning that the person wants to get out. When we say we are 'trying to get out' of something, this usually means telling a small, inconsequential lie, rather than truthfully stating that we don't want to come to work, or attend a particular party.

However, fidgety gestures including foot tapping, restlessness, jingling coins and so on can equally denote an effort to increase energy and arousal. An impulsive, extroverted person may require high levels of excitement in life and constant movement of some part of the body denotes slight boredom, and a desire to be somewhere more stimulating.

The truthful trunk

Posture tends to be more sincere than gesture, because it is more instinctual and universal. Gestures vary from culture to culture, and person to person. They are affected by social criteria, personality types, gender and age. The posture of someone who is not being honest becomes unnatural and forced.

For example, when we are aroused mentally or physically, we assume a more erect posture than when we are bored or depressed. Even people with perfect posture tend to slump a little when they are not giving their whole attention to something. A liar's posture is often stiff and controlled, for as he or she holds back the truth, honest physical expression is being held back as well. This conflict prompts an increase in body shifts – most noticeable in children who will frequently squirm about when they are being dishonest.

Research shows that when people are trying to deceive, they are less likely to touch or sit very close to you. They may actually turn their whole body away, in an attempt to conceal both their face and the truth. People also give you 'the cold shoulder' when they are rejecting you and what you are saying. When someone does this, and pretends to agree with you, you may be certain that he or she remains unconvinced underneath.

Further postural language which frequently conflicts with the spoken word may be seen socially. When people would like to leave, their bodies reveal their intentions long before they actually depart. It has been observed that during the last half-an-hour of a visit, people gradually move towards the edge of their chairs, in readiness. Of course, politeness dictates that unless we know someone very well we cannot go abruptly as we did when we were children. So we silently signal our desire, and hope that the message is understood.

Giveaway gestures

Next time you're feeling suspicious about someone's sincerity – watch the person's hands, for there are various ways in which hands can point out the truth. When we are talking normally, we tend to use hand signals to emphasize, underline and amplify the meaning of what we're saying. But when we are lying, these simple gestures are noticeably reduced in number – because the hands could, and sometimes do, contradict the lie. So people will thrust their hands into their pockets, clasp them firmly together, or clench them into a fist. Many lies are attempts to cover up negative or aggressive feelings, and these gestures often reveal when these feelings are being suppressed.

Another reason for keeping the hands under control is to prevent what has been called the 'hand shrug'. In this gesture, the hands are rotated to expose the palms – which denotes helplessness. Here the hands are saying, in effect, 'This is nothing to do with us'. And the person who uses this gesture may be in a position where the truth cannot be told, such as when trying to reassure someone who is hopelessly ill.

While simple conversational gestures decrease, the deceptive individual will touch his or her face and head more often. Children often cover their whole mouth when they are lying, as if to conceal the source of dishonesty. But by the time we are adults, we have refined this movement and often don't touch our lips at all – choosing instead to touch our faces, noses, ears and chins. Tugging or rubbing the earlobe is a sign of uncertainty which, if performed while someone is talking, signals a lack of faith in what is being said. Similarly, rubbing or touching the eye area is an indication of doubt. Should you see someone doing this while you are talking, he or she may be having difficulty in believing you – so if you are lying, you're not being very convincing!

Pinocchio's nose grew every time he told a lie. Human beings are more fortunate, but our noses can still reveal inner conflict fairly accurately – if less dramatically. A person who is not telling the whole truth, or anything but the truth, will rub, stroke and scratch the nose more often than one who is being straightforward. One explanation is simply that the nose is very close to the mouth, and the original childhood gesture of covering the mouth has been deflected to the nose. Another ingenious reason given for this gesture is that lying increases tension, and tension could result in an actual physical itch.

However, scratching to relieve an itch and rubbing the nose from uncertainty tend to be slightly different. Self-doubt is indicated by a light touch, while itching produces a much more obvious rubbing motion. A person touching his or her nose is likely to be asking one of four questions: How can I explain myself? Do they believe what I'm saying? Is what I'm saying true? Shall I keep quiet until I've decided what to do next?

Always check to see how often the nose is touched during a particular conversation. The number of hand to face gestures is likely to increase both when someone is lying, or in disagreement with what you're saying.

Face facts

The face is the most inscrutable part of the body when it comes to lying. Because we are so aware of what our faces are doing, we find it easiest to control facial expression. But modern research has discovered that we do not have complete mastery of our visual messages – for fleeting micro-expressions accurately reflect our inner thoughts. Unless you have had training in observing these split-second expressions, they can be easily missed. But you will certainly pick them up subconsciously, and begin to feel a little uneasy.

These little giveaways occur before the brain can tell the face what it wants it to say, and are considered reliable indicators that what is being said is in conflict with the true underlying feeling. If you find you can spot them, you must also consider that conflict does not always mean someone is lying. He or she may feel under pressure, with a mind full of warring ideas or worries. Uncertainty about how to react or careful consideration of what to say next may be the cause. What you can be certain of is that the person is unable or unwilling to reveal his or her current thoughts and feelings – and is trying to conceal this from you.

Most people find it very difficult to tell a lie while looking someone straight in the eye. They will look down, look away, or glance at you briefly – if at all. Shifty eyes are traditionally untrustworthy, and a sign of deception and confusion. Again, the shifty-eyed individual may not be telling an outright lie – but may be uncertain of his or her own feelings or opinions.

Not looking directly at another person can be a means of concealing the subtle pupil signals which our eyes transmit, and over which we have no control at all. Since they expand with pleasure, and contract with dislike – as well as responding to light stimuli – you can usually tell whether someone is genuinely enjoying something, or merely pretending to. Like micro-expressions, these subtle signals seem to be subconsciously noted and acted upon – although we may not always be able to explain our own reactions. When you know someone dislikes you, but nothing in their outward behaviour has led you to this conclusion, you are probably responding to some of these almost invisible clues. Indeed, awareness of pupil signals led Chinese jade dealers to conceal them from the watchful gaze of the jade salesman by wearing dark glasses. These dealers realised that the salesmen closely observed their pupils for signs of excitement when looking at pieces of jade, weakening their bargaining power.

Suspicious speech
Words are, of course, the best liars of all – which is why the telephone is such an untrustworthy instrument. But if you ignore the content, and pay attention to how the words are being spoken you may still be able to discover the truth. According to some experts, our voices become less resonant when we are lying. When the impulse to speak the truth is being blocked, the normal voice flattens, loses its depth and becomes more monotonous because we are holding back from freely expressing ourselves. Some studies show that people talk less when they are lying, and make more mistakes in their speech. They are more likely to stutter, slur

or hesitate as they speak, unless they are practised 'fast talkers' – such as con men, who can baffle you with streams of falsehoods.

PIECING THE PUZZLE TOGETHER

Concealment is probably a better word than lying to describe the motivation behind the body language that has been described. And there are numerous situations in life in which honesty may not always be the best policy. On occasion, people may be unsure of the truth while their body language is saying 'I'm a liar'. Or they may be feeling uncomfortable and uncertain.

It is also important to consider what culture someone comes from, the personality type and situation. Some cultures, such as the Japanese, or even the British, are not especially expressive – while others are dramatically demonstrative. Each may regard the other with suspicion and dislike until they understand that the inner feelings are the same, but different verbal and body languages are employed in their expression.

Every nose-rub does not mean someone is lying deliberately. Watching guests on TV chat shows, or political discussion programmes gives an opportunity to observe many of these gestures for yourself – and gain a greater understanding of the underlying mood of the person talking. Then you can start applying this knowledge to your private life – always remembering to consider the whole picture, not just one isolated signal.

THE LANGUAGE OF TERRITORY

Personal Territory

Expert researchers have analyzed our boundaries, and come up with the following four space categories which seem to have universal application – allowing for minor cultural variations of course.

THE INTIMATE ZONE: from 0 to 30 inches.

This zone begins with the body itself, extending as far as two and a half feet from it. Friends, relatives and close associates are allowed into the outer area of this invisible space; parents, lovers and very close friends are allowed to touch you and normally break through all barriers. When anyone enters our intimate zone, changes take place in the body as we respond to his or her presence. Our heart beats a little faster, adrenalin levels increase, and more blood is pumped to the brain and muscles.

All these reactions mean that the body is preparing to act – either by running away from a hostile intruder, or by hugging or kissing someone who is loved. It is no coincidence that we often describe feelings of love or affection by saying that we feel close to someone. When people such as doctors, physiotherapists or hairdressers enter our intimate zone in a professional capacity we often find it very stressful – for we cannot be open about our basic reactions, and are unable to respond one way or the other. This is perhaps why people will stay for years with the same doctor or dentist, even travelling miles to get there, rather than subject themselves to the stress of allowing a stranger into their intimate zone.

THE CASUAL OR PERSONAL ZONE: from 18 inches to 48 inches.

Here is the standard social zone, which is observed at drinks parties, in offices, and at most social gatherings. It allows us to talk comfortably to other people without feeling threatened, and we occupy it in most situations where we have just been introduced, don't know people very well, or are uncertain about them. 'Keep your distance', 'stand-offish', and 'back off' are all phrases which apply to this zone, as well as to the intimate area closer to the body. You are likely to feel frustrated, for example, if someone you like persists in keeping you 'at arms' length', and will wonder why he or she doesn't like you. Similarly, when someone you hardly know stands a little too close for comfort you will also experience confused reactions, for your primitive self will be thinking, 'Is this the beginnings of a sexual advance, or is this person about to attack me?'

Invading a near-stranger's personal space is a very dominant thing to do, however well-intentioned – and must be conducted in stages. If you go to a very crowded party where you know few people, you may find it difficult to relax and be yourself, for there is a tendency to cut off under such circumstances. Starting a conversation with people you have never met before takes courage and self-confidence. So does standing alone with your drink. Dinner parties are much easier to cope with, because the table itself provides a clearly-defined territory for everyone – and each person literally knows his or her place. A table also provides a ready-made shield which conceals the tell-tale language of legs and feet, allowing each guest a certain amount of privacy. Glass-topped tables are much more stressful because they reveal the lower body, which is the part of you that tends to be much harder to control, and will invariably demonstrate your real feelings – especially after a couple of glasses of wine.

THE SOCIAL ZONE: from 4 feet to 12 feet.
This zone is occupied by strangers, including people such as shopkeepers and workmen, TV repairers, window cleaners or others who have entered your home.

THE PUBLIC ZONE: over 12 feet.
This is the space used for performances – the audience is seated at least twelve feet away from the stage, lecture platform or action area of the sports arena. But when performers step into the audience, as they do in many modern stage productions, we find it quite disconcerting – for they are breaking the unwritten rules, and we don't know how to react to the invasion. Members of an audience, or group of students, often find it acutely embarrassing to be singled out from the safety of the crowd. For crowds seem to have a mentality of their own.

As we have seen, everyone inhabits a personal space bubble. And these invisible extensions of the body have a language all their own, which is responsible for a great many of our thoughts and feelings. For although it is invisible to the naked eye, this bubble is just as real as the radio waves which relay information around the globe twenty-four hours a day. Every living creature is surrounded by a force field of bio-magnetic energy which generations of mystics have called the aura. A number of eminent scientists in Europe and America have now developed special photographic techniques which have enabled them to produce pictures of this force field, and take the first steps towards researching its purpose and meaning.

The force is with you

A simple way of discovering your own force field is to create a closed circuit by holding your hands, palms facing each other, in front of your chest. Begin with the hands about a foot apart, making sure that they are relaxed and slightly cupped. Now slowly bring your hands towards the centre, inch by inch, until they are four inches apart. Slowly separate them again until they are back in their original position, and continue with the exercise until you feel energy building up between your hands. It will feel rather like an invisible rubber ball, and you may experience some tingling in your hands and arms.

You can also have some fun with a friend or partner once you have discovered your own energy. This exercise is most effective if your partner is naked, or wearing flimsy clothing. Ask your partner to lie down, relax, and close his or her eyes. Now place your hand, palm down, three inches above your partner's body and begin to move it around until you feel the energy. Now stop moving your hand, and ask your partner to guess where it is.

This may be easier than you would imagine, for our force field reliably transmits information to us all the time, even though we are often unaware of it. Most people 'know' when someone is staring at them, even when that person is not in their line of vision, because they feel it. So you can see that your space bubble is not just a psychological phenomenon, but can be likened to an insect's sensitive antennae. And many of your more obvious and visible demonstrations of body language result from the subtle messages supplied by the force field around your body.

Space invaders

Author Julius Fast tells of a personal experience which proved to him how disconcerting territorial invasion can be. Lunching with a psychiatrist friend one day, he found himself growing ever more uncomfortable, but was unable to identify where these feelings were coming from. All this time his friend was gradually moving his knife, fork, bread plate and cigarettes threequarters of the way across the restaurant table. Finally, the friend leant across the table to emphasize a point he was making. By this time Julius Fast was so uneasy that he was barely able to concentrate on what was being said – and so the psychiatrist relented, and proceeded to explain his actions.

What he had demonstrated so successfully was an aggressive territorial challenge, which he had accomplished by 'invading' the space of his friend. Unspoken and often unconscious rules dictate that a space such as a restaurant table is divided down the middle, and shared equally between the diners. By crossing this invisible barrier, the psychiatrist was acting in a threatening manner towards his friend – who responded with confused feelings. The moral of this story is that we all need our space, and it can sometimes be measured in inches.

HOW TO TELL WHEN YOU'VE GONE TOO FAR

Since our needs for space vary a little from person to person it can be very easy to make mistakes. Long before asking you to leave verbally, or moving away, people will use body language. So to avoid unwittingly upsetting others it is helpful to be aware of the signals used to silently communicate unease.

● Look for DISPLACEMENT ACTIVITIES such as foot-tapping, crossing and re-crossing of the legs, and general restlessness. Your companion could be bored, but could also be subtly telling you to back off. Try moving away a little, or if you are sitting at a table, steer clear of the invisible central barrier line and try not to lean across it. If you are boring somebody, the stationary dance will continue – but if it stops you will know that you were a little too close for comfort.

● Watch the EYES. Are they looking at you directly, or do they frequently glance away or close completely? This kind of eye language is telling you that someone needs time to think, may be feeling confused, and perhaps literally is not pleased to see you.

Very shy people often have trouble looking directly at others, and also have difficulty in communicating – so if their eyes are registering distress in this manner you may be dealing with an extremely introverted character.

● DEFENSIVE GESTURES are also saying 'Don't come any closer' – and this applies to both mental and physical territory. If either your questions, or your body are unsettling someone, he or she may suddenly cross arms to form a barrier between you. A subtler variation of this is crossing the body with one arm by fiddling with a watch or bracelet, or resting one arm upon the opposite leg when sitting down. Crossed legs may also point to a defensive attitude – but remember to check other gestures too.

● A need for more privacy can be revealed by changes in POSTURE. Hunching up the shoulders is one of the postures associated with fear – in this case, a person is afraid that you will completely invade his or her personal space bubble and the posture is a self-protective one. Lowering the chin towards the chest is also a way of withdrawing from you.

ORIENTATION
or, it's not what you do, but the position you do it in

Did you realise that where you decide to sit not only says something about your personality, but can also actively affect the reactions of others? The angles which are formed between people, whether they are sitting, standing, or lying down can be symmetrical or asymmetrical, horizontal or vertical. So the study of orientation is the study of the angles which invisibly connect people. Learning about orientation can help you organize more productive meetings, increase your chances of making new friends, and enhance your social life, for it is one of the foundations of positive body language.

For or against?

Sitting directly opposite another person can result in the opposition being more than physical. For whether you are playing a game of cards, having a meal, or conducting an interview, sitting face-to-face encourages competitive feelings. Of course, many restaurants seat people opposite one another partly for practical reasons, and partly to encourage a quicker turnover of customers.

But try to avoid sitting like this when you want to establish rapport, or need to negotiate. Should someone deliberately select this position for a meeting, you will have advance warning that he or she may be feeling unco-operative or aggressive. It is a useful position to adopt when you need to dominate a situation, or want to have a discussion which is short and to the point. And for added effect, seat your opponent with his or her back to an open space, or a window – while you sit with your back to the wall.

The primitive caveman in us reacts very badly to the idea that something or someone could creep up on him from behind. Subconsciously, as research has shown, we become stressed by such ancient danger-signals and our heart beats faster, and breathing rate, brain waves and blood pressure increase, reliably indicating that part of us is preparing to fight or flee.

Taking sides
The most co-operative and helpful position you can choose is to sit next to someone. It signifies trust, for you are unable to watch their every move or look at them intently. Side by side, you are equally supportive and able to work well together on a joint project or a balanced exchange of views – as long as you are not seated too closely together. There must be enough room for each person to move their body freely, or defensive postures and gestures will take over and spoil everything.

If you are contemplating buying a sofa, for example, you would do well to splash out on a three or four seater. Two people will rarely sit together willingly on a small sofa – unless they are lovers, or parent and child. A more generous seating arrangement allows for sympathetic conversations to take place between you and your friends – and will also promote exchanges between strangers.

Cosy corners
Another positive position to use is the diagonal one. Sit at right angles to your companion at a square, or rectangular table, so that the corner of the table is between the two of you, providing enough of a barrier to allow both people to feel protected. It is also very difficult to become overtly territorial in this position, for neither of you can easily act aggressively towards the other. So sit diagonally whenever you want to help someone relax, put your ideas across successfully, or conduct a friendly interview.

The eternal triangle

When arranging the seating either at work, or at home, you can make constructive use of orientation techniques to help achieve a relaxed atmosphere. By placing chairs at a slight angle to each other but minus a table, you can create an open triangle – the two chairs forming its base, while its apex might be a good position for a focal point such as a coffee table, or fireplace. When two people are seated in this way, they are inclined to talk freely and will look at each other more often – thus increasing the amount of nonverbal communication between them. Similarly, try to position two sofas in an L-shaped formation. This will help your guests, family or colleagues avoid unneccessary feelings of confrontation which could be stirred up by sitting opposite each other.

Diametrically opposite

A singularly uncommunicative seating permutation at a rectangular table is the seat diametrically opposite the other person, which is guaranteed to reduce co-operative discussion to a minimum. It cannot be a coincidence that this phrase also refers to views which are 'diametrically opposite' to our own.

You can often see people choosing to sit in this position in a library, when they don't want to be disturbed. Other public places such as cafeterias or canteens will also provide examples of this kind of orientation, especially when people are alone. And when people have been seated like this at a table with others, they will find it difficult to sustain much of a conversation – even if they were attracted to one another before they sat down. You can use this ploy if you find yourself eating with a group of people, one of whom irritates you.

TABLE SETTINGS

What kind of table do you have at home? And what shape do you instinctively prefer? Obviously, the size and shape are dictated to a certain extent by both the space available and financial considerations. But assuming you could have whatever you liked – what would you choose? The answers can be quite revealing.

● ROUND TABLES are the most democratic choice, for each person has an equal amount of territory – and no-one can dominate. It is unusual to find them in offices, or in families where one of the parents plays a dominant role. Round tables have feminine connotations and have the effect of encouraging conversation, relaxation and sharing.

By extension, circular arrangements are as old as humanity itself – appearing in ancient dances, and tribal settings. When you need to make everyone feel important, and create a welcoming atmosphere, circular seating arrangements can make all the difference between a stuffy formal event, and an enjoyably relaxed occasion. Curves are very appealing, and help people lower their territorial barriers. King Arthur's legendary round table is an excellent symbolic reminder of the democratic power inherent in the circle.

• SQUARE TABLES are masculine, formal, and suggest a closed group of people who'd rather be left to their own devices. If four people are seated at a square table, each of them will automatically find him or herself in the competitive position with another member of the group. This is slightly ameliorated by two pairs of co-operative corner arrangements – but a square table does not promote lengthy discussion or increase the desire to share information.

• RECTANGULAR TABLES AND OVAL TABLES can be used to reinforce authority, for whoever sits at the head of this kind of table wields the most power – even if everyone was equal before sitting down.

The head of the table is the traditional position allocated to the head of the family, chairman of the board, or any kind of group leader. And whoever comes next in order of authority will invariably sit to the right of the leader – indicating that the phrase 'right-hand man' is not just a figure of speech, but an instinctive recognition of power structures. The person to the left is third in the pecking order, and those with the least influence sit furthest away from the most dominant group member.

Look around your family, the next business meeting you attend – or anywhere else where rectangular tables are in evidence – and you will be able to spot those in positions of power quickly. If you are the head of the table you can expect the most opposition from the person opposite you at the other end, so it would be wise to seat an ally there if you are chairing a meeting, for example. Some people further emphasize their power by sitting in a high-backed chair, while other members of the group are relegated to smaller, less imposing seats.

Stand and deliver

Do you have difficulty in being decisive? Then try vertical orientation – in other words, think on your feet. Studies reveal that whether your body is horizontal or vertical can influence the way you think. And standing up has been shown to facilitate the kind of thinking which results in action. Quick, definite decisions are much more likely to occur when you are standing up – indeed, some management consultants recommend that short planning sessions are conducted in this way. And many people instinctively walk about when they need to reach a decision, rather than sitting and brooding.

Horizontal help

But when you need to use your imagination or jog your memory try lying down instead. Experts researching into human thought processes have found that the horizontal position can encourage reflection. And lying down also helps you to deal with new ideas, enabling you to look at all the possibilities and respond positively and constructively. Perhaps this is why many people are inspired with creative solutions to their problems while they are lying in bed – a number of famous authors write in bed too. However, you may meet with some resistance if you try to introduce this idea into the average office!

In conclusion

Initially, understanding the meaning and use of space and orientation may seem complicated and daunting. But the best way to learn is by observation, and you will soon realize how much we are all affected by these considerations. By using some of the suggestions and experiments in this section, you should be able to make more creative and effective use of your body language both at home and at work.

COPING WITH CROWDS

Travelling to work, shopping in busy supermarkets, and generally going about your daily life are all demanding activities – for you are inevitably exposed to crowds of strangers, all of whom are providing you with a great deal of information. It has been estimated that in dense crowds each person has from six to eight square feet of space in which to move, increasing to ten square feet in looser groups. But whichever kind of crowd you find yourself in, you are surrounded by a lot of other people. And if you paid as much attention to other commuters or shoppers as you do to your friends and lovers you would not be able to lead a normal life. The information overload would be so intense that you would be likely to suffer a nervous breakdown.

Adapt and survive

Since we can only absorb and digest a certain amount of information at any one time, we have developed ways of restricting the quantity we actually allow ourselves to receive when we are in a crowded place. We do this in a number of ways to lessen the impact of an abundance of data. Firstly, we speed things up by allocating less time to each new piece of information, and each person we encounter during the course of our day. In crowded cities, for example, it is very unusual to linger for a chat with the postman, or pass the time of day with the local grocer – yet this would be normal behaviour for someone living in a small country village. This kind of behaviour has given city dwellers a reputation for callousness, which they really don't deserve for they are only responding to deep-seated natural instincts.

When is a person not a person?

Indeed, all over the world we have created a virtually unacknow-ledged race of people. These people have been called 'non-persons', and are those whose existence we virtually ignore, such as newspaper sellers, street cleaners and ticket collectors. Non-persons also include waiters, milkmen and other delivery people. Few of us are reluctant to open the door to such people clad in our dressing gowns – but would probably be slightly embarrassed to greet a friend in such casual clothing.

Similarly, people carry on the most intimate and revealing conversations in restaurants, behaving as if the serving staff were both blind and deaf. And taxi drivers claim to have seen most things happening in the back of their cabs. But perhaps the most extreme historical example of the race of non-persons is to be found in ancient oriental erotic art which depicts copulating couples blithely disregarding their servants, who are usually shown bringing in some light refreshments.

STRAIGHT TO THE HEART
Unravelling the mysteries of love and attraction

Millions of words, hours of music and miles of film have been inspired by the enigma of love – and we still don't truly know what it is. Love, it seems, resists analysis. Myriad attempts to define this contradictory emotion have resulted in myriad definitions, many of them contradictory. Yet, according to one survey, 75 per cent of people gave a close, loving relationship as their reason for living. And 90 per cent of men and women have been willing victims of what Oscar Wilde termed a 'temporary insanity' at least once by the time they are 20.

THE RHYTHM OF LOVE

If music be the food of love, play on. . .'
Twelfth Night, William Shakespeare.
To get back to origins, our sensitivity to sound, which can play a considerable role in sexual stimulus, dates back to the womb. Melodies which match the heartbeat are soothing and comforting for they echo the very first sounds we heard inside the womb. Our bodies respond to rhythm in various ways. If musical tempo is slower than the human heartbeat, generally 72 beats per minute, it builds up suspense and anticipatory feelings. Ravel's Boléro is a famous example of music that produces these effects irresistibly. When the speed increases and overtakes our heartbeat, tension mounts in the body and excitement is felt – which explains the popularity of throbbing rock 'n' roll and disco music, especially during courtship.

By noticing what kind of music is being used in films you will soon be able to hear the mood a composer had in mind, and understand the powerful effect of sound on the emotions.

Poets and writers grappling with love's mysteries have reached an astonishing variety of conclusions. Love is a sickness, a frailty of the mind, the wisdom of fools; love is blind, mischievous, capricious. And, of course, it is all these things and more for there are many types of love which combine different elements and produce different relationships.

THE TYPES OF LOVE

Broadly speaking, the types of love have been divided into six categories – and most loving relationships contain elements of each:

EROS is the name given to physical, romantic and erotic love. Erotic lovers believe in love at first sight for they are strongly influenced by physical attraction. Those tentative first kisses and caresses hold special meaning for them too, as they are very sensual and place great emphasis on love-making.

LUDUS refers to the flirtatious, games-playing type of love full of teasing and light-hearted affection. Ludic lovers do not take themselves or their partners seriously and will break up a relationship if they feel it is becoming too intense. Casanova is a good example of a ludic type, for whom the game and the chase are everything. Once the final surrender has been achieved and the possibility of exploring further arises, you will not see your ludic lover for dust.

STORGE is the kind of love which blossoms from a close friendship, and is a caring, respectful emotion fuelled by shared interests and activities. These people will not seek passion and excitement, but concentrate on building an equal partnership.

MANIA is self-explanatory, for manic lovers experience violent mood swings and high anxiety levels. At their most extreme they are obsessive, jealous and dependent. Othello's destructive love for Desdemona epitomizes the kind of love which leads to crimes of passion and to suicide.

PRAGMA is realistic and practical. Decidedly unromantic, pragmatic lovers coolly assess a potential partner's attitudes, background and beliefs before taking the relationship any further. The arranged marriage is firmly founded on a belief in this kind of love, which, while lacking in drama, is certainly a sensible basis for a long-term relationship.

AGAPE is the final category and refers to the kind of love which transcends the ego and the body to reach selfless heights. The woman who devotedly nurses an elderly parent or handicapped child exemplifies agape, which is altruistic and spiritual in its highest manifestation.

When you fall in love

Whichever mode of love predominates in your relationship at any given moment, the physical symptoms are unmistakable. The poets were right – for this extraordinary emotion does produce actual physiological changes in the human body.

In one scientific survey it was found that by injecting people with adrenalin – which causes the heart to beat a little faster – and then exposing the person to an attractive member of the opposite sex, some of the sensations of falling in love were mimicked. A number of the subjects of this experiment actually thought they *had* fallen in love because of the chemically induced excitement they felt.

Addicted to love

Love can be addictive – and that's official. People in love produce increased amounts of a neurotransmitter called phenylethylamine, a brain chemical that creates the feeling of euphoria commonly associated with falling in love. This stimulant also makes the heart beat faster and increases arousal. By increasing the permeability of the blood vessels, it helps to create the flushed, rosy glow often seen on the faces of lovers. Large amounts of phenylethylamine can heighten our response to the world about us – and enable us to see colour more clearly, hear sound more sensitively, and generally feel we've been reborn.

Understandably, these delightful sensations are addictive – and according to research carried out by Dr. Michael Leibowitz lovers do, in fact, become addicted. When levels of phenylethylamine drop, people suffer withdrawal symptoms remarkably similar to those caused by amphetamines. However, there is some comfort for the broken-hearted. Chocolate has been found to contain chemical stimulants similar to this natural euphoric which act as mood elevators. This partly explains chocolate addiction, and chocolate binges as an antidote to depression.

Love is blind

'Love looks not with the eyes, but with the mind,
And therefore is winged Cupid painted blind.'
A Midsummer Night's Dream, William Shakespeare.

Cupid is indeed often depicted wearing a blindfold, shooting his arrows of love in the most unlikely directions. Despite the increased amount of mutual gazing which takes place when we are in love, what is actually seen by the eyes is edited and embroidered by the brain. Dr. Michael Brenner set up an experiment involving young couples, during which he asked them to watch a series of ordinary activities being acted out first by their partner, then by a stranger. When the participants were tested afterwards they were all able to remember the stranger's performance more accurately than their partner's. The conclusion reached was that the more powerful the emotion, the greater the memory distortion.

Liberation and commitment
When we succumb to an attraction, we are risking a great deal. Advances in contraception and the removal of stigmas associated with sexual relationships have meant that in many societies the entire process has speeded up. However, with the grim spectre of AIDS and other venereal diseases causing many people to revise their standards of morality, we may well return to a more responsible romanticism.

Commitment, implying the establishment of a loving bond, can be more sexually liberating than any number of casual liaisons. This view can be backed up by body language, for true intimacy requires that we absorb and analyze a great deal of nonverbal information about each other before we feel safe enough to become close. The term 'falling in love' suggests the loss of control we experience when falling over physically; and the French have long referred to orgasm as 'the little death' because of the total release and temporary disappearance of the ego which accompany the heights of ecstasy.

Although courtship rituals differ from culture to culture, and even person to person, the steps are identical the world over.

TWELVE STEPS TO HEAVEN
1 THE FIRST SIGHT of another can stir up very powerful feelings. It is during the first four to five minutes of visual contact that we form long-lasting impressions. We assess sex, stature, body shape, age, colouring, mood and status during these brief moments – and sometimes this information is so seductive that we fall in love at first sight.

2 EYE CONTACT further increases the amount of excitement and amplifies the information we've already received. The kind of eye signals transmitted tell us whether the other person finds us attractive, and unconscious pupil dilation reliably indicates pleasure. Gazing into each other's eyes begins to break down barriers and reassures people in love that they are loved in return.

3 SPEECH is much more than language. We are affected by the sound and tone of the voice which conveys to us impressions about someone's character and mood. A voice lacking in resonance, for instance, sounds flat and suggests a boring person. Someone speaking in a monotone will naturally sound monotonous. Yet a lively range of tonal expression will lead us to attribute vitality and positive qualities to the person. For just as we are affected by music which creates certain moods, so what we are hearing in the voice influences our perceptions.

4 THE FIRST TOUCH is usually dictated by social convention. It may be a formal handshake or the equally formal but warmer social peck on the cheek. When two people know they are attracted to each other this first touch is fraught with nervous anticipation. Will it be rejected? Will it be misunderstood? But because the urge to touch and be touched is so strong, this hurdle must be overcome if the relationship is to progress any further. Frequently this touching is disguised in some way, so that, should it be rejected, no-one loses face – after all, a helping hand across a busy street, or an invitation to dance, may be quite innocent.

5 AN ENCIRCLING ARM is placed, tentatively at first, by one person around the other. Normally, this stage is reserved for men – and traditionally this exploratory arm round the shoulders happened in the back seat at the cinema, where the darkness could hide any embarrassment.

6 HUGGING or mutual embracing follows on very quickly and completes the invasion of personal body space initiated by Step 5. This is when trust begins to become very important, for we are allowing our body to touch another's and this makes us vulnerable. However, none of the stages so far is any different from the kind of interaction we have with family members or close friends.

7 KISSING each other on the lips crosses the boundary between platonic – or non-sexual – affection, and sexual love. And, of course, such an exchange is an unmistakable way of demonstrating attraction. If kissing is prolonged and erotic it can lead to an advanced state of sexual and emotional arousal in men and women. Once this has happened both partners know that they are about to pass the point of no return. Yet in many circumstances and cultures this stage is prolonged – sometimes for months – without leading any further than the next step.

8 CARESSING the head and face demands almost total trust because they are such vulnerable areas. This is one reason why a visit to the dentist or hairdresser may be viewed with dread, for you are allowing a stranger to touch you in very sensitive places without any reassuring preliminaries. From these caresses we progress to touching and stroking the whole body.

9 ADVANCED CARESSING develops when we explore our partner's skin, which in some people is so sensitive that it constitutes an erogenous zone covering their entire body. This stroking of the skin may be likened to the massage movement called effleurage, which encourages trust, relaxes and gives sensual pleasure.

10 KISSING BODY AREAS other than the lips raises the temperature both literally and figuratively. Such loving behaviour serves to increase the giving and receiving of affection, and usually leads to specific kissing as the male partner kisses his lover's breasts. Kissing and sucking are inextricably linked with babyhood and help to strengthen bonding between two people.

11 STIMULATION of, and attention to, each other's genitals precedes full intercourse – except in circumstances where inhibition prevents this. But those who believe that sexual intercourse was designed simply for procreation have missed the point, for mutual pleasure plays an important part in joining a couple together. Since the human baby remains a helpless infant for so long, it is essential that couples stay together to nurture and protect their progeny – and sexual love creates a powerful motivation to stay together.

12 SEXUAL INTERCOURSE takes place and the couple are fully united. Usually this leads to male orgasm – essential for the fertilization of the ovum – but not always to female orgasm. Much controversy surrounds the vexed question of female orgasm, which is a sensation that varies enormously from one experience to another and can be brought about without intercourse ever taking place. This explosive form of sexual release does not seem to serve any procreative function in women and still mystifies scientists as a result. Indeed, the clitoris contains as many nerve endings as the penis – and no other animal possesses an organ whose sole function is to provide sexual pleasure.

BODY LANGUAGE AND FLIRTATION

There has always been a 'language' of flirtation. As Charles Dickens observed in *The Pickwick Papers*: 'Mingled with these groups were three or four match-making mamas, appearing to be wholly absorbed by the conversation in which they were taking part, but failing not from time to time to cast an anxious sidelong glance upon their daughters, who, remembering the maternal injunction to make the best use of their youth, had already commenced incipient flirtations in the mislaying of scarves, putting on of gloves, setting down of cups, and so forth; slight matters apparently, but which may be turned to surprisingly good account by expert practitioners.'

An understanding and knowledge of the unconscious body language of courtship and flirtation can substantially increase our chances with the opposite sex and improve long-term loving relationships by increasing levels of communication.

Pet lovers and birdwatchers are fully aware of the courtship behaviour of the creatures they observe. A pair of courting pigeons, for example, will act out a detailed little ritual which resembles the human equivalent in many ways. The male bird puffs up his feathers and struts up to the the female, accompanying his little dance with continual cooing. The female bird often turns her back on him, displaying a wounding lack of interest in his manly exertions. Eventually, she will capitulate – ensuring the future of the pigeon population on her particular window ledge.

An ability to recognize courtship signals and respond to them in the appropriate way is, therefore, an essential qualification for adult life and love.

Ready for love

The first sign of attraction seems to be an unconscious action over which we have little control and was given scientific credibility by Dr Albert E. Scheflen. He states: 'People in high courtship readiness are often unaware of it and, conversely, subjects who think they feel active sexually often do not evince courtship readiness at all. Courtship readiness is most clearly evinced by a state of high muscle tone. Sagging disappears, jowling and bagginess around the eyes decrease, the torso becomes more erect, and pot-bellied slumping disappears or decreases.'

It is logical to assume that if your body is already slim and well-toned, you will automatically seem more desirable than a sagging seductress or pot-bellied Romeo, for you are continually displaying an apparent willingness to play the courtship game. Many seriously overweight people are very insecure sexually, and are often unable to lose surplus flesh until they feel at one with their bodies.

Male courtship gestures

Just as the male peacock fans out his magnificent tail feathers, so a man begins to preen himself at the approach of an attractive woman. He will smooth and straighten his clothes, adjust his tie, pat his hair into place and often thrust his chin forward. He refrains from cooing like a pigeon, but in all other respects he is doing everything he can to make a good first impression. And recent research indicates that the first four minutes of an encounter are crucial, for it is during this time we make our minds up about another person – a decision which is hard to change and accounts for love at first sight, as well as that indefinable sensation of instant dislike.

A sexually aggressive male will then adopt the classic cowboy pose and insert his thumbs into his belt – either both hands or just one. In this way his fingers point directly at his genitals in a very obvious manner, especially if he's wearing tight-fitting jeans. This stance is accentuated by standing with the legs a little further apart and thrusting the pelvis slightly forward – a posture used to electrifying effect by singer Elvis Presley. His trouser-splitting pose, combined with a suggestive grinding of the hips, earned him the nickname 'Elvis the Pelvis'.

More restrained individuals stand with their hands on their hips, a gesture which risks looking rather effeminate. The most subtle version of this is a hand inserted into a jacket or trouser pocket; although the hand is obscured by fabric, it is pointing the way nonetheless. A quick survey of advertisements for men's suits and jackets will reveal a high percentage of hands in pockets or belts – emphasizing the masculinity of the garments and diverting attention from the sometimes effete appearance of the models.

Body pointing

Once a man is sitting or standing close to a woman who has excited his interest and curiosity, he will employ body pointing – often unconsciously – to show the direction his thoughts are taking. Next time you're standing in a group of people at a party look down at their feet. One foot will be acting as a reliable indicator of interest in one particular member of the gathering. Of course, this is not always sexual – especially in single-sex groups – but denotes an interest in what one person is saying, or a sympathy towards them.

When a couple are getting to know each other they will point their bodies towards one another, forming a barrier against instrusion by a third party. Again, in a group situation it may only be the lower body which points while the upper half remains socially available to other people present. Should you be interested in someone whose body remains resolutely pointed away from you, especially if it is towards the nearest exit, you are unlikely to get much further.

Female courtship gestures

'It's a sort of bloom on a woman. If you have it (charm), you don't need to have anything else; and if you don't have it, it doesn't much matter what else you have.'

What Every Woman Knows, Sir James Barrie.

Women have a much greater courtship repertoire available to them, possibly because men are less sensitive and need more obvious encouragement. No matter how beautiful, a very inhibited woman whose body language is minimal is making herself unattractive because she is erecting such a barrier against friendship that many men and women will give her a wide berth.

Some female gestures follow the same pattern as male gestures – they pat their hair, rearrange their clothing and direct their feet and body towards someone who has captured their interest. Now that women also wear trousers, they have adopted the aggressive thumbs-in-belt gesture which may be seen whenever a woman feels especially confident.

Resting one hand on the hip is more feminine, and centuries ago was the characteristic gesture of the sacred prostitute. In ancient Rome one of the three vestal virgins, who were believed to be wisdom incarnate, was always shown veiled, with her right hand resting on her hip.

The Indians went even further and believed that 'passion resides in the woman's right side during the bright fortnight of the lunar month, from new moon to full. The reverse is the case during the dark fortnight. The shifting of passion is believed to take place by the action of light and darkness.' (Ananga Ranga).

Sculptures of Indian dancing girls often depict them with one hand on the hip in the traditional pose of the sex initiatress inviting intimacy.

Arms and legs

Pushing back long sleeves to expose the delicate skin on the wrist and turning the palms outward towards the desired man are typically feminine gestures indicating interest. This movement is often seen in smokers and in women who play with their earrings while flirting. Fingering or stroking objects such as pens, glasses and parts of your own body are very obvious symbolic signals to an interested observer. These gestures are often blatantly exaggerated by erotic dancers and strippers.

Body language experts have observed three basic ways of sitting which women adopt when they are drawn to a man. The first of these involves pressing the legs firmly against each other while they are crossed at the knee. This emphasizes their shape by tensing the muscles and was a pose much used in pin-up pictures during the 1940s and 1950s. A much more relaxed position is when one leg is tucked underneath the other – the knee of the folded limb will reliably point in the direction of the male who is exciting interest. Women will also cross and re-cross their legs much more slowly than usual, drawing attention to their legs as they do so. If they are really aroused they will find themselves stroking their thighs, or allowing one shoe to partly fall off the foot and gently pushing their foot in and out of its casing.

Taboos

Nowadays, when women frequently wear trousers, they will sometimes sit with their legs apart, but this position still remains primarily a male preserve and there are still deep-rooted taboos in our society against females adopting this particular signal. In Victorian times women could not even ride a horse astride, but were expected to sit side-saddle encumbered by voluminous riding habits.

The open-legged position is also used by cabaret dancers to symbolize a predatory sexual mood, but interestingly they often straddle a chair and use its back as a sort of improvised shield, thus taking the sting out of the implied sexual threat or promise. However, a woman standing in a group of people may well stand with her legs a little farther apart than usual if she finds herself very attracted to one of its members. You can often see this somewhat defiant stance in fashion photographs, where it's used to make clothes look sexier than they really are, in pop videos or any other medium that aims to portray the woman as an aggressively sexy being, rather than a passive object of desire.

THE LANGUAGE OF THE FAN

Serious flirtation has lost a great ally in the fan, for it was used extensively in Europe during the 18th and 19th centuries to great effect. Originally developed in Spain's strictly-chaperoned society, it's use soon spread throughout Europe. Special fan-language textbooks were written and there was even an academy in London devoted to this subtle form of social semaphore.

Here are some of the meanings and movements:

Placing fan near heart: 'You have won my love.'

Pressing half-opened fan to lips: 'You may kiss me.'

Placing fan behind head: 'Do not forget me.'

Placing fan behind head with little finger extended: 'Goodbye.'

Fanning very quickly: 'I am engaged.'

Fanning very slowly: 'I am married.'

Touching tip of fan with finger: 'I wish to speak to you.'

Covering left ear with opened fan: 'Do not betray our secret.'

Hiding eyes behind opened fan: 'I love you.'

Drawing fan through hand: 'I hate you.'

THE LOOK OF LOVE

'Drink to me only with thine eyes,
And I will pledge with mine;
Or leave a kiss but in the cup,
And I'll not look for wine.'

To Celia, Ben Jonson.

When trying to determine whether or not someone is attracted to you, their eyes can provide the answer every time, for they speak a subtle, sensitive and highly revealing language. The decisions we reach when observing an interesting person or a beautiful scene are processed by the brain almost simultaneously – and, as all artists are aware, each individual perceives what he sees in a different manner.

The great French artist Henri Matisse, spoke eloquently of this process in a conversation with his friend, André Marchand: 'Do you know that a man has only one eye which sees and registers everything: this eye, like a superb camera which takes a minute picture, very sharp, tiny – and with that picture man tells himself: "This time I know the reality of things," and he is calm for a moment. Then slowly superimposing itself on the picture another eye makes its appearance, invisibly, which makes an entirely different picture for him.

'Then our man no longer sees clearly, a struggle begins between the first and second eye, the fight is fierce, finally the second eye has the upper hand, takes over and that's the end of it. Now it has command of the situation, the second eye can then continue its work alone and elaborate its own picture according to the laws of interior vision. This very special eye is found here,' Matisse said, pointing to his brain. (*Matisse on Art*, J. Flam).

Most people are familiar with the confusing mixture of sensations aroused when someone stares fixedly at them, because this can signal either hostility or fascination – and sometimes it's very difficult to distinguish between the two. But when it comes to love and attraction natural fears are evident in the way we look at each other, and for how long. Painfully shy people experience great difficulty looking directly at others, a trait noticeably exacerbated by feelings of attraction. They are unable to gaze into the eyes of the beloved, and instead steal covert glances from beneath their lashes. When Princess Diana was just learning to

overcome her adolescent awkwardness and cope with the barrage
of attention from the Press, she frequently gave just such a look at
the cameras.

Teenagers in particular are often reduced to staring helplessly at
their feet, for they are so overcome with emotion and unfamiliar
sexual longings that any further distraction would be unbearable.
This kind of overwhelmed reaction was amusingly personified by
Walt Disney's cartoon dwarf, Bashful, who was hopelessly in love
with Snow White and made 'sheep's eyes' at her whenever she
spoke kindly to him.

Gazing

The effectiveness of the gaze when signalling interest in another
was graphically described in an old witchcraft manuscript, where
knowledge of body language seemed to be just as important in the
art of fascination as more arcane abilities: 'For when your eyes be
reciprocally bent one upon the other and are joined beams to
beams and lights to lights, then the spirit of one is joined to the
spirit of the other and strong ligations made and most violent love
is stirred up with a sudden looking on, as it were, with a Darting
Look, or piercing into the very inmost of the heart. . .'

It is this holding of the gaze just a little longer than necessary
which is one of the first signs of attraction. Should the person
delivering this look also possess what are popularly known as
'bedroom eyes', then the message will have double impact. The
Chinese describe these eyes as 'peach blossoms', likening them to
the sensuous beauty of the peach, while the Spanish philosopher
José Ortega y Gasset spoke of 'the most effective, the most
suggestive, the most delicious and enchanting' look. He was
referring to the alluring heavy-lidded look which many consider to
be the most seductive, and further describes it as '. . . the look of
eyes that are, as it were, asleep but which behind the cloud of
sweet drowsiness are utterly awake. Anyone who has such a look
possesses a treasure.'

Many actors and actresses have employed this look to create a
sexy image, often aided by dark eye make-up – an indispensable
piece of equipment for the femmes fatales of the silent movie era.
And Omar Sharif, Robert Mitchum, Sylvester Stallone and Clark
Gable are all masculine exponents of bedroom eyes, proving that
they are big box-office.

Dilated pupils

Most people know that the pupils of their eyes respond to light and dark by dilating and contracting. But, irrespective of prevailing light conditions, they also respond to emotion in this way, expanding with pleasure and contracting with distaste or repulsion. This is one piece of body language we can do nothing about because it is unconscious. Centuries ago Italian courtesans would use belladonna, obtained from deadly nightshade, as an artificial pupil dilator to make themselves more attractive – so a knowledge of pupil signals is nothing new.

Babies display an inherent ability to use their eyes to speak for them. Almost from the moment they are born their eyes will follow the direction of sound or voice – and they are naturally blessed with such large pupils that their gaze cannot help but be appealing. Again, the cartoons of Walt Disney provide excellent examples of the powerful 'love me, I love you' message delivered by huge pupils. Try to imagine Bambi without his huge black discs but with pin-point pupils instead and you will realize how much we are all affected by this signal. Indeed, villains and monsters are usually portrayed with tiny pupils, often surrounded by an unnaturally coloured iris which accentuates this – and may partially explain why snakes and reptiles are hated and feared, while the large-pupilled owl is often perceived as endearing and sweet despite being a carnivorous bird of prey.

Automatic responses

When a mother looks at her baby her eyes become moister, softer, and the pupils enlarge. Even women who are childless will normally respond this way to the sight of a baby, as will men who are fathers. Men who genuinely dislike children, and who have never had any, show the opposite reaction when faced with a baby – their pupils contract with distaste.

This automatic response has even been used to reveal unexpressed racism; in one experiment a group of self-styled liberals were shown pictures of black people kissing white people. Some 'liberal' members of the group were unable to hide their prejudices when their pupils contracted at the sight of a mixed race couple in love, while the eyes of those who were genuinely pleased by evidence of racial harmony displayed the opposite reaction.

Another classic exercise involved two pictures of the same

attractive girl, but in one of the photographs her pupils had been retouched to appear dilated. These pictures were shown to an audience, and the men were asked to indicate which picture appealed to them most. Without knowing why, nearly all the men chose the girl with enlarged pupils. These men were acting on attraction signals which they were able to discern unconsciously. And while the pupils of heterosexual men and women reliably expanded when shown pictures of naked members of the opposite sex, homosexuals of both sexes only responded to their own sex.

Experiments with 'Casanova' type males revealed that such men do not react normally to pupil dilation, preferring instead pictures of girls with small pupils – a signal of unavailability. Their delight in the chase and fear of involvement were so deeply-entrenched in their characters that they preferred women who seemed to be unattainable and unloving.

Personality indicators

If you think someone is interested in you, you can also discover their basic personality type from the way they look at you during conversation. When two people are talking to each other they don't spend the entire time looking directly into their partner's eyes, but break the gaze in some way to reassure the other that they are friendly, not hostile. Therefore, those who extend their gaze and stare at you unblinkingly are behaving in a dominant way, a trait which could be difficult to cope with in a long-term relationship. A rapid scanning of the other's face shows an excitable personality, probably enthusiastic about life and love and impatient as well.

Another telling movement to watch out for is the direction of the gaze once initial eye-contact has been broken. Does the person look to their left or to their right? Research suggests that those who break their gaze to the left seem to be creative, imaginative and intuitively inclined; people breaking to the right are much more structured in their approach, logical and numerate. These findings tie in with what is known about the left and right hemispheres of the brain, each of which performs a different job. The left hemisphere controls the right side of the body, and specializes in language functions, analysis of information and rational thought. The right hemisphere, controlling the left side of the body, is nonverbal, creative and visual.

A KISS IS JUST A KISS

'The following are the places for kissing: the forehead, the eyes, the cheeks, the throat, the bosom, the breasts, the lips, and the interior of the mouth. Moreover, the people of the Lat country kiss also the following places: the joints of the thighs, the arms, and the navel. But Vatsyayana thinks that though kissing is practised by these people in the above places on account of the intensity of their love, and the customs of their country, it is not fit to be practised by all...Kissing is of four kinds: moderate, contracted, pressed and soft. Different kisses are appropriate for different moods.' *Kama Sutra*.

The kiss is a universal expression of affection and love. Between lovers the first mouth-to-mouth kiss signals the beginning of an intimate relationship. In the East kissing is regarded as so intimate an activity that it is still very much restricted in public, and was not seen in Indian films until recent years – when it caused much controversy. Although we no longer have such strictures in the West, a deep-rooted acknowledgement of the power and meaning of kissing still lingers in our behaviour, as shown by the fact that few prostitutes will kiss their clients. According to the British Marriage Guidance Council, kissing between unhappy couples ceases before lovemaking does. It seems that men and women find it easier to copulate than to kiss.

Powerful chemicals
Kissing is addictive. Lovers and poets have always known this, but scientists have now endorsed the romantics' beliefs and proved that chemicals have as much to do with it as Cupid. When we reach puberty special sebaceous glands develop at the edges of the lips and inside the mouth. These glands produce semiochemicals which are transmitted by close touching between two people, enhancing and stimulating sexual desire. And the more you kiss, the more sensual semiochemicals are released, thus heightening both the desire to kiss and the attractiveness of our kissing partner.

Biological memories
Anthropologists explain kissing in an even more unromantic fashion, for research shows that deep erotic kissing involving both

lips and tongue is actually a modification of mouth-to-mouth feeding. Originally, mothers would chew up their baby's food and then pass it directly into the infant's mouth. This kind of feeding is still performed by Papuan women, although it disappeared long ago in the West. And even now babies instinctively push their lips forward from the age of about three months indicating that they are still biologically adapted to receive nourishment in this way.

Our shadowy tribal memories linger on – couples in love often share the same piece of fruit, and the ancient Indian sex manual, the *Kama Sutra*, recommends passing wine from one mouth to the other as part of love-play.

Kissing and health

Your dentist could well recommend kissing three times a day after meals because extra saliva – which kissing promotes – washes food particles off the teeth, lowers acid levels in the mouth and helps prevent build-up of plaque, a major cause of tooth decay. And slimmers will be pleased to learn that every kiss uses up three calories. However, to lose half a kilo in weight you would need to kiss 1,000 times . . .

Yet there are drawbacks for those aiming to live to the age of 100, for every time you kiss up to 250 assorted germs pass between you and your partner. The 'kissing disease' mononucleosis is often contracted by teenagers experiencing their first love affair. If you're a kissing addict suffering from swollen neck glands and constant fatigue – see your doctor. Recent American research states that passionate kissing can even shorten your lifespan. Because kissing has the same effect on the body as stress and causes the heart to beat faster, it's claimed that every kiss shortens your lifespan by three minutes. The choice is yours!

Strengthening bonds

Kissing is undoubtedly a very important part of a loving relationship. Sometimes we associate it with our teenage years, with the beginning of a love affair, or with being childish. Yet it would be a pity to relegate this delightful piece of body language to the back seat of a partnership once the initial ties have been formed. By including more kissing in an intimate relationship you can strengthen and even improve it, benefiting both yourself and your partner and enhancing the emotional rapport between you.

WHAT'S YOUR KISSING STYLE?

Eyes open – or closed?

Although 97 per cent of women close their eyes while kissing, only 30 per cent of men do so. It has been suggested that women feel the sensations more strongly and lose themselves in the moment, whereas men are more stimulated by the sight of their loved one.

Cuddle – or crush?

Those who indulge in gentle cuddling while kissing reveal a sensual, affectionate nature. They are loving, uninhibited and sexually confident, and probably received lots of tactile attention as babies.

Lovers who try to crush you very tightly to them – as in the classic romantic fiction hero who 'crushed her to his manly chest', are in fact basically insecure. Male clutchers are often fearful of revealing their softer side and seek to give the impression that they are in charge.

Selfish – or sensual?

Puckered and closed lips are signposts pointing towards inner blocks. Just as the eyes are said to be the windows of the soul, the mouth is a gateway. Should that gate be permanently shut against the outside world, you are dealing with someone who is rejecting part of themselves. This rejection of intimacy revealed by closed lips probably has its roots in childhood and signals a fear of abandonment and an inability to let go and give without counting the cost.

However, the person who begins with a series of short closed-mouth kisses and then progresses to longer lingering ones, is extremely passionate and sensual. Such lovers will make up their minds in their own time, but when they do they will wholeheartedly commit themselves to a relationship and enjoy exploring their partner mentally and physically.

Those who engage in 'French' kissing, or kissing involving the tongue, seek to create a powerful and intimate bond. And this type of kissing is probably the best way to do it, combining as it does the exchange of bonding chemicals and the deeply rooted ancestral memories of babyhood. This type of kisser has a generous nature.

Nibbles – or bites?

Use of the teeth when kissing – be it gentle nibbling or real biting – indicates yet another link between nourishment and love-making. This erotic equation finds its expression in the popular myth of the glamorous vampire of either sex whose victims swooningly succumb.

THE LANGUAGE OF SCENT

'I have been here before,
But when or how I cannot tell;
I know the grass beyond the door,
The sweet keen smell,
The sighing sound, the lights around the shore'
Sudden Light, Dante Gabriel Rossetti.

Evocative, with the power to conjure up forgotten memories, to seduce, or to disgust, our sense of smell is often not consciously taken into account. Much like the subtler signals received by our eyes the information scent gives is acted upon subliminally. Yet as part of the unspoken exchange of body language our natural scents still play an important part in attracting or repelling others. Phrases like 'she came up smelling of roses', 'the sweet smell of success', 'I smell a rat' and 'he's got a nose for it' all reveal an awareness of this primitive ability which, nowadays, tends to be obscured by confusing layers of perfumes, deodorants, skin creams and clothes.

Signals from the skin

Polynesians, Eskimos and Lapps all rub their noses together as a sign of greeting and affection which enables them at the same time to smell each other's skin and thereby make the distinction between 'friend or foe'. This practice is so ancient that it is mentioned in a text from the pyramid of Teti in Egypt: 'Geb rejoices at thy approach; he extends his hand to thee; he kisses thee; he fondles thee.' The word used here for 'kiss' is 'sn', which is ancient Egyptian for 'smell', symbolized by two noses, tip to tip.

In 19th-century Fiji smelling formed part of the natives' farewell ritual, as related by one Mr Johnson, in his book *Camping Among Cannibals*: 'One or two of them then took my hand and smelt it, making rather a noise about it, which is here a very courteous and respectful method of salutation and farewell.' Among some tribes in new Guinea a similar custom survives to this day. When a much-loved friend or relative is about to leave on a journey those being left behind press their hands into the armpits of the traveller, and rub the smell into their own bodies for a distinctive memento which lingers long after the loved-one has gone, and is much more intimate than a photograh.

Natural scents

We spend millions annually on perfumes, after-shaves and deodorants to make ourselves more attractive, when nature has provided us all with our own unique scent signals. When a baby is just two weeks old it recognizes its mother by her special smell, and during the first weeks of lactation the mother secretes a scent which seems to repel men, thus ensuring that while the baby is at its most vulnerable it can rely on the total attention of its mother.

In adult life we develop scent glands under our arms, on the breasts and around the genitals – and the body hair which appears at puberty helps to trap these scents and spread them further. It is clothes which turn the smell of healthy sweat into an unpleasant, acrid odour by trapping it and causing it to go stale. However, Napoleon was one man who relished an unwashed aura, for at the height of their romance he would send orders to Josephine which read 'Home in three days – don't wash.'

Novelist H.G. Wells, an unprepossessing little man, was very attractive to women. An extremely puzzled friend of his once asked one of Wells's mistresses why she found him so beguiling, expecting her to enthuse about his intellect and humour. She replied simply: 'His body smells like honey.'

Pheromones

Scientists investigating our sense of smell have found that, in tests, all women are able to detect male scent, but the ability to detect a woman's scent varies in men. A woman's sense of smell is also tied up with her menstrual cycle, reaching its lowest level during menstruation and becoming most acute at the time of ovulation. Research conducted in an all-male prison in America demonstrated that the presence of an ovulating woman had a definite effect upon prisoners – so much so that the governor advised women to schedule their visits accordingly since the men would be 'more disturbed than usual' after such a meeting.

Such subtle sexual scents are called pheromones. They are found throughout the animal kingdom and are also employed by moths to attract a mate. Certainly the American Indians were well aware of the aphrodisiac power of male scent and exploited this in some of their ritual dances by seating their women downwind. As the dancers whirled and stamped with increasing frenzy their recognizably male scent was wafted over the female audience.

A great deal of controversy surrounds the question of human pheromones and the part they play in dating and mating, but some interesting experiments seem to indicate that they do affect us. Male pheromone is called androsterone and is secreted from the sweat glands and in urine. Female pheromones – copulins – are related to vaginal secretions and increase at ovulation.

Two experiments involving androsterone produced thought-provoking results. In the first, half the seats in a theatre were sprayed with it; most of the seats were then occupied by women. The second experiment was made in a telephone booth in Euston Station, London. The booth was duly sprayed and, out of the row of six, it was then used by more women than any of the others.

Hair colour and scent

A French researcher, Professor A. Galopin, has refined scent definition even further by claiming that a woman's natural hair colouring alters her body odours. Redheads smell of violets, brunettes exude a musky perfume and blondes are reminiscent of ambergris. Another Frenchman, novelist J.K. Huysmans, also had definite ideas on the subject of female smells: 'Daring in brunettes, sharp and fierce in redheads, in the blonde it is subtle and heady, like some "flowery" wines. . .'

Not many men are so perceptive, and women have used perfumes for thousands of years to emphasize their presence. However, it seems that men would be well advised to take note of feminine sensitivity in this area and abandon after-shave in favour of the alluring scent of their own skin.

THE LANGUAGE OF CLOTHES

What you wear, and when you wear it, affects everyone who sees you. Personality, political inclinations, occupation, sexuality and even religion are all suggested by what you wear. And whether you like it or not, your clothes make a strong visual statement about how you see yourself. Indeed, since research has shown that we tend to look at the body before making eye contact or speaking, body shape and clothing – which can influence body shape by shifting emphasis to different parts of the body – can have considerable impact. In his book, *Style in Costume*, fashion historian James Laver described clothes as 'the furniture of the mind made visible'. By observation you will realize this statement's truth.

SMALL, MEDIUM OR LARGE

The body beneath the clothes makes the first statement to others, for research has shown that rightly, or wrongly, we attach different personality traits to different body types. These have been broadly classified as ectomorph, mesomorph, and endomorph.

Slender, bony ectomorphs are thought of as introverted, highly-strung and sensitive; muscular mesomorphs are independent, well-balanced and outgoing; and fat endomorphs are generally believed to be kind, jolly and dependant. Of course, there are many variations in these types – and bodies change with age; a mesomorph can gain weight or an endomorph successfully slim down. Genuine ectomorphs, however, are unlikely to alter much with time – although regular exercise could fill out their muscles a little.

WHY DO WE WEAR CLOTHES?

Protection, modesty, status and magic have all been proposed as reasons why human beings wear clothes. And the motive is probably a mixture of all four, since these criteria still exist today.

Protection from the elements is perhaps an obvious reason to most of us, but when Charles Darwin explored wet and windy Tierra del Fuego he observed that the natives were naked – but decorated themselves with body paint and feathers. And the remaining primitive tribes of the world only dress up for special events in their religious calendars, going about nearly naked the rest of the time.

Modesty is another, apparently obvious, reason which is subject to question. Erogenous zones have shifted throughout history, as have standards of female modesty. Tudor dresses, for example, were stiffly padded and elaborately decorated hiding the shape of the body beneath – yet some of them were cut down in the front almost to the nipples, as surviving paintings reveal. Even prim and proper Victorian ladies showed off a startling amount of cleavage in the evenings, combined with submissively sloping shoulders. The general effect was that of a fleshy flower emerging from a heap of fabric – too delicate to do very much but look decorative.

Anthropologists suggest that because our sexual organs are at the front of our bodies we instinctively cover them, to avoid sending constant sexual messages to our fellow human beings. The proverbial fig-leaf, they argue, was the first item of clothing to come – and will always be the last to go, even on permissive beaches. Ironically, a girl in a well-cut swimsuit usually gets more glances than one clad in a skimpy bikini-bottom – simply because the one-piece succeeds in creating an air of mystery, however slight this may be.

Status and magic are close companions. By dressing for success, or to create an impression, we are invoking one of the basic principles of all magic – to affect events according to our will. Much thought goes into choosing an outfit for an important interview, a first date, a wedding or a funeral. And many outwardly logical people possess a pair of lucky socks, a special tie, or swear by the dress which never fails to get results. Scratch the surface of civilization, and you'll find that we all have a good deal in common with the witch doctor who dons amulets and ankle bracelets, or with the fairy-tale hero in seven-league boots.

THE BAROMETER OF FASHION

Changes in prevailing styles, skirt-lengths and emphasis on different parts of the body are believed by some historians to reflect both the society we live in, and our roles within it. Female emancipation during the 1920s neatly coincided with the fashion for a boyish silhouette, short skirts and short hair. Women were symbolically freeing themselves from constriction – although many of them had to bind their breasts to achieve modishly flat chests, another kind of constriction altogether.

There is some evidence to suggest that hem-lines do reflect economic conditions – rising with financial bouyancy, and descending when a recession strikes. During the course of the 20th century, short skirts have certainly reflected boom and bust with astonishing accuracy – most obviously during the 1960s era of the mini-skirt, which rapidly lengthened to sweep the ground during the depressed early 1970s.

Similarly, the female waistline acts as a social barometer. When it shifts to an unnatural position – such as below the waist, or under the bust, it is said to indicate social change. At the time of the French Revolution the waistline rose, creating the 'Empire line' dress which echoed classical Greek dress. And during the great social upheavals of the 1920s it dropped to the hips.

Our most recent revolutionary decade, the '60s, saw fashionable female waistlines wandering all over the place – only to settle back in the normal position with the recession in the 1970s. It seems that in financially uncertain times humanity requires women to exert a stabilizing influence – by looking like women. When everything is in the melting pot, women are free to experiment with the shape they present to the world.

How old are you?

Our clothes also signal mysterious changes in the age we want to be. During the 1950s it seemed that everyone wanted to look like a mature 30-year-old – clothes were responsible, sober, sophisticated and adult. But by the mid-'60s, we were all dressed as if we were on our way to kindergarten – sporting vivid colours, splashy prints, and huge collars topped by heads of hair which, like small children's, were disproportionately large in relation to the body.

Fashion no longer dictates such universal looks, but raids the past and traditional ethnic costumes for its inspiration. Perhaps this indicates a world made smaller by travel, and an acceptance of the value of individuality.

Clothes talk

So-called 'power dressing' is simply a successor of ritual tribal dress, for it seeks to imbue the wearer with influence. From elevator shoes, through military uniforms to exaggeratedly padded shoulders, people seek to enhance their body language through clothing. By increasing height and width, we hope to increase our ability to dominate, and attract attention – just as a bird fluffs out its chest when courting, or an angry cat erects its fur.

Modern clothes consultants echo the advice given centuries ago by Greek philosopher Epictetus, 'Know, first, who you are; and then adorn yourself accordingly.' But he could easily have said, 'know where you are, and the image you wish to project' – for there is nothing more unfortunate than allowing your clothes to say the wrong thing at the wrong time.

A woman who wishes to be taken seriously as an executive is usually told to wear a suit in order to blend in with the men she works alongside, or who work for her. Similarly, a man in jeans and a sweater is perfectly acceptable to society if he is an artist, workman or enjoying some free time – but put him in a conventional office environment, and few people would take him seriously. The primary function of clothes may well be to protect us from the elements and cover our nakedness, but these simple examples demonstrate the powerful effect our clothes can have – far removed from such practical considerations.

MALE SEX SIGNALS
Male clothing signals fall into two broad categories – gender enhancement, or sexual advertising, and clothes which represent financial security, maturity, and – crudely-speaking – husband material. Nowadays, male sartorial sexuality is somewhat restricted, a far cry from the days of the imaginatively padded codpiece, or thigh-hugging stockings which men once wore as a matter of course. However, tight jeans and unbuttoned shirts remain possible avenues of display – and there is always status-dressing as compensation.

A well-cut suit, an immaculate uniform, or expensively-tailored leisure clothes suggest male dominance, assertiveness and the ability to provide. They are also representative of adult responsibilities and commitment. Men who habitually dress like this are fundamentally conformists; while those who prefer brightly-coloured shirts, no tie, and casual separates are peacocks or rebels. Many men conform all week, and rebel at weekends or on holiday – but this may be seen as a backward glance to the more carefree days of youth, when they could dress casually all the time.

FEMALE FASHIONS
Women have a wider range of images available to them – dictated only by fashion, income and shape. This may reflect the many roles a woman has to play in the course of her life, especially today when countless women are working mothers.

Modern female shoulders are broadened by both exercise and shoulder pads, symbolically suggesting a woman who is built to shoulder the burdens of life. Women are also free to dress like men in most social situations without attracting the controversy which would surround a man in the same circumstances.

Many women appear even more feminine dressed in a jacket and trousers, while successfully demonstrating their ability to 'wear the trousers'.

The extraordinary taboos which once existed against females in trousers have faded as feminism has become more acceptable. But women are still advised to wear a skirt for important interviews, and Britain's Prime Minister, Margaret Thatcher, has never been seen wearing trousers in public – although members of the Royal Family have, with sport or, in the case of Princess Diana, youth, to 'excuse' them.

The sensual wardrobe

Other hidden messages may be found in the texture, fit and colour of clothes. There is nothing very sensual about a neatly-buttoned suit made from synthetic material – but a flowing, jewel-coloured silk shirt with a few buttons left undone at the neck would project quite a different image.

Indeed, tightly fastened clothes do seem to suggest closed minds and a buttoned up sexuality – unless the garments are deliberately figure-hugging and therefore erotic. When someone loosens a tie, undoes a jacket, or otherwise relaxes standards of dress in your presence it is a sign that the person feels he or she can confide in you – and is literally opening up.

ACCESSORIES

Hats, umbrellas, ties, shoes and handbags are all common accessories which, according to psychologists, speak volumes. To begin at the top, hats add authority because they add height – 'If you want to get ahead, get a hat' was one old advertising slogan which encompassed this message. But in recent decades the hat has fallen on hard times, and is no longer a *de rigeur* accessory. Instead, it is generally relegated to weddings, formal events, eccentrics and business-men.

Sporting caps, knitted balaclavas and head scarves seem to represent the last line of defence – but there are many people who would never consider wearing them, preferring to go bare-headed. Possibly this indicates a more egalitarian society; it certainly undermines the clothing-as-protection theory.

Ties and umbrellas are favourite Freudian phallic symbols. And whether or not you subscribe to this theory, a tightly-knotted, shabby little tie will never enhance any man's virility. A well-designed, warmly coloured tie with a large knot sends out a more positive manly message, although it may also indicate egoism and vanity if very brightly coloured. A man's umbrella, too, should never be damaged, small or past its best if its owner wishes to impress others.

Bags and shoes are symbolically female, and are therefore more significant in female wardrobes. The high-heeled shoe is feminine because it causes women to take smaller steps than flat footwear, and accentuates the natural sway of a woman's hips as she walks. Very high heels also exaggerate the leg's shape, making it look sexier. Another advantage is that heels add height, and therefore power – at a price, for they render their wearer quite helpless; it is very difficult to run while wearing high heels.

Because of their womb-like interiors, bags are a classic symbol for the female gender – have you ever heard a man referred to as 'an old bag'? This is a telling phrase indeed, for some psychologists link female sexuality with female handbags – and they could be right. For just as men rarely carry small, tatty umbrellas if they are confident – neither do women carry battered old handbags through choice, unless their self-image is badly in need of boosting. Small, tightly shut, neat bags are also off-putting – signalling repression and frigidity.

THE LANGUAGE OF BODY DECORATION

Modern make-up may seem to be sophisticated – but it isn't really very different in essence from ritual tribal adornment. We still decorate ourselves. And although nowadays male face-paint is left to rock-stars, actors, and assorted exhibitionists, there are other forms of body decoration, such as tattoos, for Western 'natives' to choose from.

In tribal societies, body decoration reveals an individual's status, gender, and often age, for it frequently forms one of the rites of puberty. Tattooing and other forms of permanent decorative mutilation say 'I belong', and are ways of making the human body more appealing and individual. Elaborate tattoos also serve the same function in the West, proclaiming an ability to bear the pain of the needles, plus membership of a special group of risk-takers. On the whole, tattoos are permanent reminders of an impetuous moment – usually experienced during the early twenties or adolescence.

Body piercing is another echo of our tribal past – men and women have been piercing ears, noses, and other parts of their anatomy for thousands of years. At the height of the punk era thousands of young people pierced their ears and noses, decorating them with chains and safety pins in an effort to outrage more conventional adults.

There was also a passing vogue for multiple holes in the ear, demonstrating an ability to display lots of earrings. This kind of body decoration is, like much 'clothing display', one of the ways we use ornaments to advertize our wealth, self-image, and place in society. In other words, we're still telling interested observers which tribe we belong to . . .

FACE PAINT

Historically, face and body paint had magical, mystical links with spirits and gods. People painted themselves before hunting, or making war on another tribe – and also decorated their skin to attract luck, love and fertility into their lives.

Sometimes make-up was also used to protect delicate parts of the body from the elements. The Ancient Egyptians, for example, painted their lower eyelids with kohl to protect them from the fierce rays of the sun. This practice is still followed in North Africa, India and Afghanistan. Then along came status – for being able to decorate yourself is a sure sign of having the time to do it. And time not only equals money, but also hints at a lifestyle where mundane tasks are performed for you by others.

Today, make-up still retains elements of all these ancient criteria. Why, for instance, do millions of women use red lipstick? The answer could have a lot to do with sex and fertility – two symbolic meanings associated with the colour red. Some tribal women in New Guinea paint their whole face red, because scarlet means fertility to them. Using red lipstick seems to subtly echo this message.

Cosmetic advertizing is also full of magical sounding suggestions, hints and promises. Use our products, the advertizers say, and you'll be beautiful, powerful, desirable and so on. Judging by the amount spent on make-up every year – we believe them.

BEYOND THE PALE

Status is still with us too. Long nails, elaborate eye make-up, false eyelashes and diamond-studded teeth have all been inspired by a wish to show off wealth, time, or belonging to a special group. But the suntan is probably the best modern example of this, for its status value has been very much part of the 20th century – and for a number of reasons its power is now on the wane.

Until the 1920s, a suntanned skin said 'Poor, manual worker toiling in the fields'. Wealthy people went to great lengths to avoid exposure to the sun – covering themselves up, carrying sunshades and staying inside. But the Industrial Revolution slowly changed all that as more and more people worked in factories to earn a living, and rarely saw the sun.

Enter the Beautiful People who suddenly decided that it would be fun to spend the summer soaking up the Mediterranean sun. Influential figures like Pablo Picasso and Coco Chanel broke with convention, turned brown, and started a trend which has now spawned a multi-million pound industry. And now most working people regard a fortnight in the sun as normal, the suntan is gradually losing its appeal.

Health warnings about the danger of sunbathing are only part of the reason for the suntan's demotion – a suntan may now be acquired without any travelling at all, and it has become common. As with every trend, once something has lost its hard-to-acquire status it's no longer worth having.

THE LANGUAGE OF HAIR

The powerful symbolism of hair winds its way through thousands of years of history. Perhaps no other part of our anatomy has been subject to so many changes, decorations, substitutions and superstitions.

WOMEN'S HAIR

Hair is closely linked with sexuality for both men and women. Many religions forbid women to display their hair either in public, or in places of worship. This is because it is believed to incite base desires in any man who sees it. Such taboos still apply in many parts of the world, and may also be indications of the fear and distrust female sexuality can arouse.

Conventionally, a long-haired woman is thought to be sexier, warmer, and more available than her short-haired counterpart. But this was not always the case. During the French Revolution, and the 1920s, short hair on women indicated daring, unconventionality, and an independent spirit.

Nowadays, when anything goes, short hair may mean a tomboyish attitude; a love of neatness; radical political beliefs; or a rejection of some of the more traditional aspects of femininity. It can also look extremely feminine, in the same way that male clothing worn by a woman can enhance her female qualities.

However, if a woman who has always had long hair cuts it off, this is a reliable signal that she is undergoing major changes in herself. These changes are deep-rooted, and if the woman is in a serious relationship can signal her discontent with this state of affairs. Sometimes a dramatic change of image precedes a divorce, change of career, or other big turning-point.

Similarly, dyeing the hair a totally different colour also indicates a big shift in self-image – or a restless desire to create change. Our ideas about the characteristics of blondes, brunettes, and redheads may seem superficial. But on many levels we believe them. These beliefs are constantly reinforced through television, magazines, advertizements and films – so that we all have to think very hard before realizing that they don't always apply.

Blondes, brunettes and redheads

Blondes are supposed to have more fun. They are eye-catching, frivolous, sometimes funny, or delicate. Alfred Hitchcock had a weakness for icy, self-controlled blondes whose cool detachment masked criminal tendencies or a vortex of bottled-up emotion. A blonde woman can be an obvious status symbol for a man, or a feather-brained bimbo. Blonde hair is usually associated with flirtatious natures,and a light, playful sensuality.

Brunettes, on the other hand, are normally thought to be basically serious. Their seriousness and intellectual abilities may also be combined with powerful emotions, and a passionate nature. Brunettes are more likely to succeed at interviews than blondes because we associate this hair colour with maturity, stability, and intelligence.

Redheads can be as frivolous as blondes, or as sensual as brunettes depending upon the exact shade of red. Deep, coppery auburn tones suggest tempestuous passions, while lighter golden red shades are associated with a sharp tongue, satirical wit, and rebellious qualities. All redheads are supposed to have a temper.

These colour codings also apply to men. Male blondes, however, have a much harder time than females. Blonde men are less likely to be taken seriously, for we associate this colour with children particularly and often view men with blonde hair suspiciously. Many comedians are blonde, and this seems to fit in with the type's light-headed image. But in other fields, blonde men must try harder to be convincing.

Dark men are often thought of as more manly, desirable, and dependable. Romantic fiction frequently makes a dark-haired man the dashing hero. Perhaps this stems from the classic stereotypes in Wuthering Heights and Jane Eyre. Dark hair says here is a man with a past, possibly strong and silent, and definitely masculine.

Red-headed men have had a very bad press. Their temper is not just tempestuous, but often murderous. Many people do not trust redheaded men, believing them to be fickle and volatile. These attributes are clearly untrue in the vast majority of cases, but the messages are still ticking away just beneath the surface of our consciousness. So never make any hard and fast judgements based on hair colour – you could be making a big mistake.

WEIRD BEARDS AND MANLY MOUSTACHES

Men may not use make-up, but they can always grow some facial decorations. Beards and moustaches seem to have a life of their own, sending out a complex set of messages to everyone who sees them. At various times in history they have proclaimed political affiliations; in Ancient Rome only barbarians had beards, by the mid 19th century beards and moustaches were symbols of authority and respectability.

Today, the message very much depends on what kind of facial hair is grown, and how it has been groomed. Untamed hair spells eccentricity – usually artistic or scientific. Here is a mind above mundane matters, set apart from the common herd. Similarly, very decorative waxed moustaches or 'Van Dyke' beards show a desire to be different. But their owners are self-conscious, possibly theatrical, and capable of planning the effect they wish to create.

Facial hair can also demonstrate a macho, or would-be macho attitude. Men who cannot or will not grow such sex signals are regarded by those who do as lacking in masculinity: 'Kissing a man without a moustache is like eating an egg without salt', or as one American cowboy put it, 'you've got to go through the under-growth if you want to get to the picnic.' Some women, however, would rather go hungry – or prefer to eat their eggs without salt . . .

Hair today, gone tomorrow

Other messages may be read into the sudden growth or shaving off of male facial hair. Why does a clean-shaven man decide to grow a beard or moustache? If he is in his early twenties, or even late teens, he is usually signalling membership of a group who also have beards or telling the world at large that he is an adult male. Later in life he is visibly displaying some new aspect of character, talent, or attitude. Maybe he secretly wants to be thought of as more serious, artistic, or unconventional.

Often he is passing through the male 'mid-life crisis' – which occurs anywhere between the ages of 38 and 50. He could be about to leave his job, his wife, or even change his politics or religion. If he keeps this new development, these changes will be permanent. Frequently, however, such growths are temporary and shaved off when things are more settled inside and out.

Bearded individuals who suddenly shave the beard off can become almost unrecognizable to their nearest and dearest. And this is probably the intention. Again, some fundamental changes, or desire for changes, are taking place in this man's life. He may long to look younger, or perhaps convince himself that he is still young enough to change his life successfully.

If he originally grew the beard as a rebellious statement he may not feel that way any more. This man is saying that he no longer needs to rebel, or has established his reputation sufficiently to be judged on that alone. Whatever the reason, change is the keyword and if you are involved with such a man personally or professionally – expect the unexpected.

WHAT IS ATTRACTIVE?

Beauty, they say, is in the eye of the beholder – and throughout history there have been some startling variations in what we consider attractive. There are also considerable differences between the sexes which are believed to stem from our primitive ancestors' roles as hunters (male) or food gatherers and mothers (female). Although this theory perhaps explains why women are attracted to men who are assertive, independent and powerful – qualities which indicate a potentially reliable provider and father for their children – it does little to clarify why, in one British survey conducted in 1985, 40 per cent of men placed physical attractiveness at the top of their list. But this is possibly connected to the fact that if we regard someone as attractive, we also credit them with a long list of other desirable qualities which they may – or may not – possess. In judging a book by its cover we automatically assume that an attractive person is also talented, intelligent, happy, sensitive, warm and outgoing, has higher status than ourselves, enjoys successful relationships and is kind.

The wicked witch of fairy tales is rarely beautiful, for her outer ugliness signals her inner evil. When an unscrupulous sorceress is portrayed as beautiful she becomes far more dangerous – the kind of femme fatale described by Keats in his poem, *La Belle Dame sans Merci*:

'I met a lady in the meads
Full beautiful, a faery's child;
Her hair was long, her foot was light,
And her eyes were wild.'

The naively trusting knight of the story is completely fooled by this ethereal enchantress, only to discover he is just one of numerous kings and princes she has ensnared.

WHAT MEN FIND ATTRACTIVE IN WOMEN

If a composite Miss World may be considered as a general indication of what Western males find irresistible then their ideal woman would be a 21-year-old blonde with brown eyes, 5ft 8in tall, and measuring 35-24-35. Fortunately for the millions of women who do not answer to such a description, this composite creature merely shows us what the average beauty contestant is like. Though a visually attractive exterior is highly appealing, by itself it does not constitute sex appeal – as any glamour photographer will affirm.

Responding to female gender signals

What are scientifically known as 'gender signals' are the physical differences between males and females which enable us to tell each other apart. By emphasizing these signals, we hope to make ourselves more attractive to the opposite sex and have a wider selection of possible mates to choose from.

A woman's gender signals are mainly concerned with demonstrating her child-bearing abilities and need for protection while rearing her children. Her pelvis is naturally broader, her waist narrower, her legs more slender than the male's. Because of larger quantities of subcutaneous fat a female body is more rounded where these extra deposits occur – most noticeably on the breasts, hips, bottom and thighs. A woman's knees and shoulders are also more spherical than a man's for the same reason. Facially, women have fuller lips, narrower eyebrows, softer skin and normally an absence of facial hair. The exaggerated wiggle in the walk of the stereotypical sex kitten is simply overstating the natural difference between the male and female pelvis, which causes women to sway slightly from side to side as they walk or run. And, most men would agree, *'Vive la différence'*.

Breast, bottom or leg men?

It has been said that men divide into breast, bottom and leg men and that these preferences give some indication as to character. For instance, men who are aroused by the sight of large breasts are sporty extroverts, while those who like smaller bosoms are intellectual introverts. Men who like women's bottoms are also supposed to be more mature than those who respond to a pair of shapely legs. Indeed, the female bottom transmits the most primitive erotic message of all – something French can-can dancers understand very well. A female ape 'on heat' will display swollen buttocks to indicate that she is fertile and ready for mating, but human females do not show any cyclical changes in their buttocks – and are consequently signalling readiness at all times.

However, there is some evidence suggesting that the remnants of a primitive attraction cycle are still operating. Women who are ovulating seem to be more attractive to men than women who are not fertile, and often experience stronger sexual sensations at this point in their cycle.

While it is possible to use the marriage of British royals Prince Andrew and Sarah Ferguson as an example of an extrovert, sporty man falling for a well-endowed lady, it is also possible to cite the example of bespectacled intellectual Arthur Miller marrying Marilyn Monroe, who could hardly be described as small-breasted. So these criteria are best taken with a pinch of salt. Even in today's diet-dominated society, where slimness is relentlessly promoted as attractive, there are plenty of men who prefer voluptuous curves. Cartoonist Gray Joliffe tells of a doctor friend of his whose tastes seem to go beyond the Rubenesque: 'He once told me he was in love with a woman who was so ample that when she lay on top of him he couldn't hear the stereo.'

WHAT WOMEN FIND ATTRACTIVE IN MEN

Ask the average man what he thinks women find attractive and he will promptly deliver a list of traditional masculine gender signals. Most men seem to believe that women like a man who is tall, muscular, has a hairy chest and a large penis. With the exception of the penis and hairy chest which simply say 'man', the big muscular macho-man symbolizes a successful hunter and, hence, provider. Visually, the majority of women do prefer a man five to six inches taller than themselves, with small muscular buttocks, a flat stomach and slim build. This may be explained partly by the fact that sexual interest causes an involuntary tensing of the stomach muscles, and a taut stomach therefore denotes attraction and excitement – appealing qualities in themselves.

Character counts

Although physical characteristics might improve a man's chances of literally bringing home the bacon, they do not indicate by themselves the character traits that women prefer. As comedienne Mae West once quipped, 'It's not the men in my life but the life in my men that counts.' In 1983 a MORI poll discovered that looks are far less important to women than they are to men – only 23 per cent of women placed them at the top of the list. Qualities such as faithfulness and personality won much higher scores, as did assertiveness and competence. In one study in which blindfolded women were guided through a maze by a male partner it was found that the women were more attracted to the man who successfully helped them through, especially if he touched them instead of just verbally assisting them.

The lure of power

'Kissing your hand may make you feel very, very good but a diamond and sapphire bracelet lasts for years.'

Gentlemen Prefer Blondes, Anita Loos.

Women are much more choosy than men when it comes to selecting a mate. The reasons for this are obvious – once a woman is pregnant, she is committed to nine months and many years of involvement with her child after that. Even women who do not want, or cannot have, children are unconsciously taking these facts into consideration when choosing a man. Thousands of years of evolution cannot be erased by a comparatively few years of feminist thinking. Since the biological differences between the sexes are not simply going to disappear, a woman's approach to sex and sexual arousal is bound to be more discriminating.

For many women power and money are greater aphrodisiacs than broad shoulders or a sexy smile. Jacqueline Kennedy didn't marry Aristotle Onassis for his physique, nor did Sophia Loren wed Carlo Ponti because he was tall and muscular. Both of these men emanated power in their different ways, and both of them were in a position to help and protect their women – much like the men guiding women round the maze.

HOW TO BE MORE ATTRACTIVE

'A thing of beauty is a joy for ever;
Its loveliness increases; it will never
Pass into nothingness.'

Endymion, John Keats.

For centuries men and women have suffered to be beautiful, hoping to impress their contemporaries, to find love and win favours and attention. Yet, without charm, a handsome man or pretty woman is unlikely to achieve any lasting success in relationships. This magical ingredient lasts a lifetime and oils the wheels of social progress in every sphere of life.

Although charm is an elusive, almost indefinable quality, it does seem to be directly connected to our interest in other people – and our ability to demonstrate that interest with body language. Positive body language can be cultivated and powers of attraction increased. Charismatic film stars are able to relate to the camera as if it were a dear friend instead of an unwanted intruder. The audience then reacts to this message and perceives that special something which is often labelled 'star quality'.

Britain's Queen Mother radiates an extraordinary amount of charm, causing people who have met her only briefly to feel as if they really mattered to her. By improving your body language in a number of ways you can elicit more positive reaction from others. When this happens your confidence grows, and what may have begun as an exercise becomes something you no longer need to be consciously aware of. People who like people are automatically likeable and attractive, for they invoke this feeling in their friends and lovers – all of whom feel more special as a result.

So which aspects of body language can you use to encourage others to find you more attractive? The following hints should help you to devise your own charm school schedule, and highlight areas where you may be lacking.

Physical appearance

While the late Duchess of Windsor claimed that you could never be 'too thin or too rich', neither of these attributes has much to do with being attractive. What is important is to be at home in your body, what the French refer to as *être bien dans sa peau* – which translates literally as 'to be well in one's skin'. It is your body, it is uniquely yours and if you don't love it how can you expect anyone else to do so?

If you are overweight you should try and do something about it for the sake of your health. However, it's more important to take regular, gentle exercise. A relaxed enjoyment of movement and a gradual strengthening of the body are more likely to help you lose weight than foolish and self-defeating crash diets. Good muscle tone is very attractive and when achieved will increase confidence in yourself.

When it comes to clothes, colour is very important, for it delivers powerful subliminal messages to the onlooker. Clear glowing colours – whether pastel or primary – are the ones to look for. Consider, too, when and where you are planning to wear certain colours – what looks fine in daylight may be altered by electric lighting, for instance.

By familiarizing yourself with the meanings of colours you can dress according to the impression you wish to create. A slavish adherence to the vagaries of fashion is unnecessary and frequently unattractive, hence the derogatory term 'fashion victim' to describe people who follow trends at the expense of both their wallet and their individuality.

Eye contact

You shouldn't be afraid to look people in the eye, but neither should you stare so long that they feel threatened or embarrassed. Using direct eye contact during conversation, if thoughtfully done, will encourage intimacy and make the other person feel that they have your undivided attention. An awareness of cross-cultural differences is also useful as the amount and frequency of eye contact do vary from one country to another.

People will naturally look at one another a lot when they are talking about impersonal subjects, and less so when the conversation veers towards more intimate or sensitive areas. But when someone is interested in your response to the subject, or likes you very much, he or she increases the amount of glances as well. You should also bear in mind that extroverts look more than introverts do, and this simple piece of information can help you determine someone's basic personality. Although the use of eye contact must always be tailored to the situation, lookers are generally perceived as more attractive people than non-lookers.

Use your head

Holding your head in an erect, but relaxed, position will help you to appear more confident and encourage trust in others. Nodding the head is an affirmative gesture we use to say yes, but it also means that we have understood and agreed with what is being said. Using slight head nods during conversation effectively demonstrates that we are paying attention and also encourages the other person to continue. Research shows that people talk up to three or four times more than usual when listeners nod their heads at regular intervals. Without turning yourself into a parody of a nodding toy dog you can greatly encourage others to speak freely by using this technique.

You can also demonstrate attention and encourage communication by tilting your head slightly to one side while listening – but again, it's vital to be subtle and avoid imitating a cute puppy when using this movement.

Nodding three times signals your desire to break into the conversation and, if accompanied by appropriate words, such as 'Well...' or 'I agree, but...' should help you make your point. Studies have shown that men nod their heads more than women while talking, as if to underline what they are saying, but women, who have a better reputation as listeners, nod their heads more often while listening to others. Experimenting with a little role reversal here could make men seem more sympathetic, women more assertive.

Voices

Talking doesn't mean just passing the time of day – it has a great deal to do with body language and timing. Timing is one of the qualities which distinguishes a good comedian from a bad one, and depends upon an alert and sensitive understanding of the myriad signals we receive from others. An ability to join in with a conversation at the right moment, to say the right things, to be interested and interesting are all traits which make a favourable impression – particularly on women.

The tone and pitch of the voice are also important. A nasal, high-pitched voice does not inspire trust, whatever the verbal content of the speech. And talking too quickly, perhaps from nervousness, literally creates the image of a 'fast talker', which is also detrimental to an open relationship. Many male and female heart-throbs of the silent movie era failed to make the transition to 'talkies' because their unattractive voices ruined their sex-appeal.

A very successful series of advertisements for an Italian apéritif featuring Cockney actress Lorraine Chase demonstrated the power of the voice to alter our perceptions. Ms Chase was dressed to thrill in an expensive evening gown, her hair was immaculately coiffed, her make-up perfect. She moved with incredible poise and grace, and didn't speak a word until the very end of this mini fantasy, when she finally opened her mouth and squawked a reply to her smitten suitor – and the sophisticated swan dematerialized before our eyes.

Smiling

It may seem to be stating the obvious, but it's true to say that 'when you're smiling, the whole world smiles with you'. However nervous or shy you are, a smile will ease most situations and normally evokes an answering smile – lightening tension and opening the doors of friendship and acceptance. Smiling is an inborn spontaneous reaction which all human beings have in common. If you smile more often at people you will find they'll enjoy your company more. Indeed, an animated face is always more interesting to behold than a stony mask.

In order to improve the mobility of your face, it's essential to free it from hidden tensions and keep the muscles firm. We are often completely unaware of our habitual facial expressions – look around you at work or in the street and observe how many frowning faces there are. After a while the muscles automatically group themselves into a permanent scowl, signalling negativity to the world at large. This kind of unguarded facial language not only affects those who see it, but research shows that it can actually influence our emotions. One experiment asked a group of people to smile; they were then shown a number of pictures of different subjects and asked to say how these images made them feel. They reported a pleasurable reaction. Then the same group of people were requested to frown before considering the pictures. They described negative feelings ranging from a mild sense of annoyance to anger.

Simple facial exercises

Your face tells the world how you are feeling, it is there to help you express yourself. Using massage and exercise you can improve the eloquence of these expressions of emotion and communicate more effectively. Your appearance will also benefit as your face will look more alive once it's freed from negative armour, which ultimately distorts the planes of the face. There is some truth in the old admonition 'Don't pull that face, or you'll stick like it'.

Jaw

A surprising amount of tension collects in the jaw as we often grit our teeth unconsciously when trying to suppress anger and severe irritation. Next time you're caught in a traffic jam, check the muscles in your jaw and up along the sides of the face where the jaw is hinged. It will probably feel solid, and if you press firmly it may be quite painful. To loosen these muscles simply move the jaw around from side to side; stick it out as far as you can; open your mouth wide and stick out your tongue, and try to exhale through your mouth as you do so. Pretend to yawn and as you do so feel the stretch.

Massaging this area will help to clear away tensions which have collected there over a long period of time. To do this you should use some oil or rich cream. Keep your fingers firm, but do not press too hard or you could cause damage – simply move the muscles around with small circular motions. You can also run your two thumbs along the jawline, hooking them underneath the bone and proceeding in a sweeping movement from the chin towards the ears.

Eyes and forehead

Anxiety and fear seem to collect around the eyes and forehead, creating some types of tension headache and ugly frown lines. Eye strain can be helped by placing your palms over your closed eyes and trying to 'see' black or deep blue. Slowly circling the eyes to the left, then to the right, is a useful exercise. And without moving your head try looking as far as you can to the right, blink, then look to the left, blink again and look up slowly and down again. These exercises will prevent your eyes becoming locked and frozen by tension, for if you consider the typical expression of fear or rage you will realize that the eyes stare fixedly in both these states. This kind of staring can make it difficult to make contact with others – it's very unappealing and does not encourage situations where feelings can be shared.

To increase mobility in the forehead, raise your eyebrows as high as you can – then feel the release of tension as you lower them. Frown hard, and again try to notice the difference in muscle tone as you release this expression. By consciously noting the physical feelings various facial grimaces call forth you should, with practice, be able to stop yourself from unintentional glowering.

In addition to specific exercises, you can experiment with your face by moving it in any direction which comes to mind. Pulling faces will not only exercise your face but also remind you just how many individual muscles it contains. Learning to use your face to express emotion will undoubtedly increase self-awareness and help you to become more sensitive when reading others' expressions.

Posture and gesture

Numerous theories exist about the extent to which our minds and bodies are linked. But what clearly emerges from research is that our posture reflects our basic personality – that is to say its underlying structure – while gestures embroider, emphasize and communicate from moment to moment and culture to culture.

For example, certain therapists will point to the position of the pelvis as an indicator of the balance between mental and sexual attitudes. A pelvis which is tucked under so far that it tilts forward is a posture often assumed by rock stars and Latin men – such a person is flaunting his gender in a very obvious way, so that his message reads 'sex first, intellect second'. Equally unbalanced is the person who retracts his pelvis, ending up with a sway-back, lower back pain and an unnaturally protruding bottom. This is very common in Western society where we place tremendous emphasis on brains, often at the expense of our bodies.

Maintaining a relaxed, upright posture is attractive because it denotes a balanced mind in a balanced body. When you are sitting down you can also use your posture to demonstrate interest and attention. Lean slightly forward in you chair, especially when listening, and the other person will normally respond by becoming more expansive. As the meeting becomes more informal and you want to relax, it's most attractive to lean back and slightly to the side, so that your partner remains in your line of vision and can still see your face. Try not to fidget as most people read this as a sign of impatience at best, boredom at worst.

Be as open as you can with your posture. Avoid tightly folded arms and legs because these barriers shut the doors of communication and suggest defensiveness rather than warmth. Similarly, when using gestures to amplify the spoken word, try to be expressive. Once you have relaxed, such gestures will come naturally – and nothing is more attractive than spontaneity.

Space and touch
This is a very delicate area because we are all sensitive about our personal space and some people find if difficult to touch or be touched, however briefly. But it's safe to assume that if other signs are positive you can move in a little closer without seeming threatening. If you receive a negative reaction then consider whether the other person is very shy, hence embarrassed by your closeness. Have you correctly gauged other attraction signals before moving in? These cautions apply to touch, too. Neutral areas of the body such as the arm, shoulder or hand are safest to begin with and unlikely to cause offence. Fleeting brushes of the hand will indicate your attraction and warmth of feeling, without introducing a sexual element too soon. And you are more likely to be remembered, for you have established a sympathetic contact.

And finally. . .
Attractive people are those who are true to themselves. Never try to manipulate others with your body language. Instead, use it to create a relaxed and intimate atmosphere. Try to forget about yourself, open your mind and body to the moment – and the moment will be yours.

128